Series

Editing and Management of Photographs

with Adobe® Photoshop® Lightroom® Classic software

Volume #1

Basic Concepts
and Workspace

J. Armando Fernandes

1st Edition

2019

Dedications

To my wife, my longtime companion, thank you for the love, friendship, and endless adventure in our life to two.

To my children for the joy, affection, and pride they have given me from the moment they were born.

To my brothers, thank you for the long and healthy conviviality since our childhoods, and friendship that never was shaken.

Special thanks:
To my father (*in memoriam*) and my mother, thank you for the outstanding affection and dedication in my education.

Copyright

To simplify the text, from this point, onwards, the term "computer software" will be replaced by the word "software."

Foreword

Over the last few years, I have worked as a photographer and image editor, using digital cameras and computer software for this purpose. Unlike older cameras with physical films, these modern devices do not require a darkroom for development, since they generate digital computer files. Digital photograph editing and management software do this task.

This new universe, in which the digital file replaces the old film, allowed to bring the old darkroom into the photographer's computer. With this change, he can now perform every step of the way from capturing photographs to the final result after editing in the post-production phase, which can be understood as the modern way of development photographs. In my case, it was no different, so I started to use a desktop application designed specifically for photographers - the Adobe® Photoshop® Lightroom® Classic software by Adobe Systems Incorporated. To simplify the text of the e-book, from this point, I will refer to the application only as "Lightroom software."

To record my experiences and studies using this software, I started writing this series of e-books, with the idea of presenting it in a complete, detailed, and strongly visual way. Thus, the volumes of the Editing and Management of Photographs series are full of pictures, screenshots and illustrations, making it possible to understand the subjects presented even without the aid of a computer with the Lightroom software installed at the time of reading. And during its use, the volumes that make up the series will serve as a reference for deepening knowledge on specific subjects. Also, along with the theory presented, several examples and tips will be available to the reader, not only regarding the use of the software but also in the area of digital photography, which will undoubtedly enrich the knowledge of professional and amateur photographers.

Although the volumes of the series are entirely focused on the Lightroom software, readers who employ another computer software for the same purpose can apply the numerous theoretical knowledge presented by adapting them to the application used. There is also a wealth of useful photography and post-production information throughout this e-book that will allow the reader to deepen their knowledge in the field. However, keep in mind that the volumes in the **Editing and Management of Photographs** series are not intended to be a photography course.

The Lightroom software is a powerful and sophisticated application for managing and editing photographs in a practical and very productive way. Despite this, its well-designed interface allows new users to access key software features with no hassle quickly. However, to explore its full potential requires dedication and study, an activity in which this e-book is intended to support.

Therefore, the main purpose of the **Editing and Management of Photographs** series, consisting of several volumes, is to convey to readers the concepts involved for the practical and productive use of the Lightroom software.

I hope the contents of this e-book offer a pleasant and enriching experience in using the software. Comments, suggestions, and criticism will be welcome. Access my author's page on the Internet and e-mail for contact in the links below.

https://jarmandofer.com

jarmando.fer@gmail.com

Useful information on photography, image editing, and new e-book releases in the series can be found on the author's LinkedIn® professional networking services page, Facebook®, Twitter®, or Instagram® at:

https://www.linkedin.com/in/jarmandofernandes

https://www.facebook.com/jarmandoescritor

https://twitter.com/@JArmandoFer1

https://www.instagram.com/jarmandofernandes

Good reading and lots of photo editing!

Organization of this e-book

This e-book is **Volume #1** of the **Editing and Management of Photographs** series, which features the first six chapters of the work:

▸ Chapter 1 - Introducing the Lightroom Software;
▸ Chapter 2 - Differences Between Lightroom and Adobe Photoshop CC Software;
▸ Chapter 3 - The Lightroom Software Workspace;
▸ Chapter 4 - Photography Workflow;
▸ Chapter 5 - Image File Formats;
▸ Chapter 6 - Lightroom Software Workflow; and
▸ Appendix - Exercise Answers.

It is recommended to read the first chapter to the last sequentially, to allow the consolidation of the basic knowledge necessary to understand all the content, as well as the other volumes of the **Editing and Management of Photographs** series, organized in eleven volumes:

▸ **Volume # 1 - Basic Concepts and Workspace;**
▸ Volume # 2 - Importing and Organizing of Photographs;
▸ Volume # 3 - Viewing, Selecting, and Filtering of Photographs;
▸ Volume # 4 - Fundamentals of Photographs Editing;
▸ Volume # 5 - Color Adjustments in Photographs;
▸ Volume # 6 - Sharpness and Noise in Photographs;
▸ Volume # 7 - Using Presets;
▸ Volume # 8 - Local Adjustments in Photographs;
▸ Volume # 9 - Increasing Productivity;
▸ Volume # 10 - Exporting and Sharing of Photographs; and

▸ Volume # 11 - Preserving of Work.

Screenshots were taken using an iMac® computer with Apple® macOS® operating system. Most of the time, they are identical in the version for computers with Microsoft® Windows® operating system. The differences are subtle and do not interfere with the understanding of the text.

Changes to this e-book will emerge over time as Lightroom software updates, released by Adobe to subscribers through the Creative Cloud® online service. They may be accompanied by the company's website at the link below.

https://www.adobe.com

I prefer to suggest you conduct a search on the site for this and other information rather than citing links here, as they may change from time to time. After a considerable number of updates, they will be consolidated into new editings of the **Editing and Management of Photographs** series volumes. Visit the author's LinkedIn, Facebook, Instagram, or Twitter pages to stay informed of the latest news and other books to be released.

After a considerable number of updates, they will be consolidated into new editings of the **Editing and Management of Photographs** series volumes. Visit the author's LinkedIn, Facebook, Instagram, or Twitter pages to stay informed of the latest news and other books to be released.

At the beginning of each chapter are presented its **objectives** to guide the reader and to facilitate reading. Some notes have been included throughout the text to broaden information on the subject. Although not essential to understanding the content, it is recommended to read it to deepen the acquired knowledge. They are preceded by the word "**Note**" as shown in the example below:

Note:

> *Note text.*

The end of each chapter has three complementary parts to the text:

- **Shortcut keys,** being presented the most important to increase productivity in the use of the software;
- **Smart Tips**, containing useful information for more practical and productive use of the software; and
- **Review**, consisting of multiple-choice exercises that will consolidate the topics covered in each chapter. In the **Appendix**, at the end of the book, are the answers for verification.

Shortcut keys and **Smart Tips** will be displayed starting from **Chapter 3**.

Table of Contents

Chapter 1
Introducing the Lightroom Software

Chapter 2
Differences Between Lightroom and Adobe Photoshop CC Software

Chapter 3
The Lightroom Software Workspace

Chapter 4
Photography Workflow

Chapter 5
Image File Formats

Chapter 6
Lightroom Software Workflow

Introduction

In recent years photography has been undergoing significant evolution. With it, new ways of capturing and processing images have been made available to professionals and lovers of this activity that mixes art with science. The most significant transformation occurred in the shift from physical film to the digital file, which opened new possibilities and definitely popularized the practice of producing photographs. Today a simple mobile phone with a built-in camera, which has become the standard in so-called smartphones, turns every user of these devices into a potential photographer all the time. And the quality of the images has become better and better due to the constant evolution of technology.

Because of this, there has been an exponential growth of photographs produced by both professionals and amateurs. In this way, new challenges present themselves, especially regarding the cataloging, storage, and editing of large quantities of photographs.

In this context, the Lightroom software can address these challenges by presenting itself as a complete solution for managing large photograph catalogs and editing them productively, facilitating organization and processing.

This e-book aims to present the features and possibilities of this software in a well-illustrated and easy to understand way, allowing its readers to master it completely. It also raises important questions about digital photography and image file formats. It compares Adobe's two leading image-editing software: Adobe Photoshop CC and Adobe Photoshop Lightroom Classic. Even the most experienced are suggested to read the e-book from the beginning to broaden their knowledge.

For the preparation of this e-book, I used the Lightroom software installed on an iMac computer with macOS operating system. However, the application is essentially the same for both Apple and Microsoft Windows operating systems users. This way, it can be used on both platforms without significant difficulties. The subtle differences, when they exist, do not compromise the use of the application or the understanding of the text. If necessary, they will be cited.

Because the Lightroom software is a sophisticated application, addressing all of its features in one e-book would make it too long. Thus, it was decided to divide it into several volumes to be published successively, allowing readers to obtain only those that are necessary for their studies. If desired, each work can be purchased together in a single e-book after the release of all volumes in the **Editing and Management of Photographs** series.

I hope you have a good read and beautiful photos to organize and edit!

Important Notes:

Chapter 1

Introducing the Lightroom Software

Knowing the main features of the software designed for photographers

This chapter will present the main features of the software and other fundamental aspects of its use, allowing a better understanding of the other volumes of the **Editing and Management of Photographs** series.

Chapter objectives:

- ▸ define the Lightroom software and its purpose;
- ▸ introduce how to get an application subscription;
- ▸ understand what the Adobe® Camera RAW software is;
- ▸ understand the concept of Non-destructive editing;
- ▸ know the end products of the Lightroom software; and
- ▸ learn about its integration with the Adobe Photoshop CC software.

1.1 - What is the Lightroom Software

The Lightroom software desktop version, of which full name is Adobe Photoshop Lightroom Classic, is a digital photo editing and management application with specific features to organize and streamline the workflow of photographers, hobbyists, and professionals alike, making them more productive.

Unlike other image editing software, it is geared toward managing and editing large quantities of photographs, with a variety of features that make this task more efficient and productive. Its **Workspace** can be viewed in **figure 1.1**.

Screenshot of Lightroom Classic software reprinted with permission from Adobe Systems Incorporated

1.1 - Lightroom software Workspace

However, it does not have some features of other image editing software, such as using layers or inserting text, as this is not its purpose. Therefore, it is not suitable for creating graphic designer compositions, such as those produced with the Adobe Photoshop CC software or other image editing and compositing application.

The limitations can easily be circumvented by their easy and efficient integration with other image editing applications, which have composition-specific features such as the Adobe Photoshop CC software. The Lightroom software is designed specifically for photographers to make their work more productive.

1.2 - Purpose of the Software

The Lightroom software aims to edit and manage digital photographs taken from multiple sources, with specific features to organize and streamline the workflow of amateur or professional photographers, making them more productive. In addition to allowing the export of photographs in various image file formats, it also can share the results of edits made on social networks, prepare files for print media, generate content ready to be posted on the Web, among many other features.

In-software photograph editing allows for various corrections and adjustments in exposure, color, white balance, red-eye, cropping, and framing, just to name a few. Besides, masks can be used to limit corrections in some regions of the picture, creating simple selections. However, unlike other image editing software, it does not allow, for example, text insertion, the use of layers, and the use of complex selections to create sophisticated compositions.

Currently, the software also can integrate with mobile devices such as smartphones and tablets, allowing you to access your photographic projects literally from anywhere.

Note:

*It is possible to put an image over a photograph like a layer using the menu **View > Loupe Overlay > Choose Layout Image**, which also has some other interesting options. If you use an image that contains only a text with a transparent background, it is even possible to put it over the picture as well. However, these tasks have a lot of limitations and can be useful only to preview and anticipate pretty simple compositions. If necessary, try to use an application specially designed to work with layers and texts, like the Adobe Photoshop software, for example.*

1.3 - Where and how to get the Software

You can only obtain the Lightroom software, for both macOS and Windows operating system users, by subscribing to the Adobe Systems Incorporated website at *https://www.adobe.com*. Click the link or type this address into your web browser and visit the page for more information.

Note:

Internet address changes depending on the country. In the example above, it is from the website in the United States of America. When in doubt as to the correct address, visit Adobe's United States page at https://www.adobe.com. If you are accessing outside the USA, a message will appear on the screen, suggesting you go to your local website with the corresponding link, if available, or continue to the USA website if desired.

To get a subscription, you must have an ID called Adobe ID, providing a contact e-mail, which will be your login, and a password to access the system. From this identification, you can purchase subscriptions for all products on Creative Cloud services.

For professional and amateur photographers, Adobe provides a one-time subscription containing both leading photo and image editing software, namely the Lightroom Classic and Adobe Photoshop CC software together, called the **Photography** plan. Look for it on the photographers' link, usually located on the subscription plans page on Creative Cloud online services. Again it may be necessary to perform a small search, as the location may vary on the site over time.

The **Photography** plan primarily includes Adobe Photoshop Lightroom Classic, Adobe Photoshop CC, and Adobe Photoshop Lightroom software, the latter a simplified version of the Lightroom Classic software for editing, managing, and sharing photographs from anywhere, accessible from desktop computers and mobile devices, such as tablets and smartphones.

In addition to the software mentioned above, other handy features for photographers are also available when signing the plan, such as the Adobe® Portfolio online platform. It allows you to create portfolios in both web browsers and mobile devices easily, and space for cloud storage on Creative Cloud services. Check the site for information on what the **Photography** plan includes, as well as other plans for more details.

If you just want to organize and edit your photographs, either professionally or for personal use, Creative Cloud's **Photography** plan is ideal. I recommend taking the time to browse the site to learn about all products and plans if you are also interested in other Adobe products.

Trial versions of other software are also available for a while so that they can be used before contracting a plan. These trial versions can be downloaded from the Creative Cloud site itself and will require an Adobe ID identifier. If you don't already have yours, create one by clicking the **Sign In** link, usually located in the upper right corner of the site, and after the **Sign In** screen appears, clicking the **Get an Adobe ID** link. Then provide the requested data, and your account will be created. You can then download the Creative Cloud application to your computer, which will manage your account, access installed applications (**Open**), access trial versions (**Try**), and store your files in the cloud, as well as countless other tasks. I suggest that after you create your Adobe ID, you download this application to follow up on the next topic.

1.3.1 - Software Versions

Unlike the old computer software selling system, where the buyer and future user did install from any physical media, the current subscription system allows installation from the Internet through the Creative Cloud online service website. From an Adobe ID, it is possible to access the subscription and all contracted plans, and then downloads of the applications belonging to the plan.

Another feature of this new software selling system, which is a significant advantage, is the automatic updates made available by the service application, without the need for new hires or acquisitions. This way, your version of the Lightroom software will always be up to date if you agree to download updates. They are automatically requested by the service when available, as long as you are logged in with your Adobe ID.

The Open command buttons in the Creative Cloud application installed on your computer change to **Update** whenever a new version of a program is available, allowing you to update it.

Also note that when the software is available for installation, an **Install** command button appears next to its name. Remember that Lightroom and Lightroom Classic software are different, although they have the same purpose.

Note:

The current Adobe Photoshop Lightroom Classic application was formerly called Adobe Photoshop Lightroom, the same name currently used for the cloud-based software, which also has a mobile version for smartphones and tablets. In this e-book, only the Adobe Photoshop Lightroom Classic software for desktop editing is being addressed and, to simplify the text, termed just like Lightroom. Notice in the Creative Cloud software on your computer that, apart from their names, their software icons are also different.

To check the version of Lightroom software you are using on your computer, follow **procedure #01**.

Procedure # 01 - Checking the Version of the Lightroom Software Installed on Your Computer

1. select **Lightroom Classic** menu in macOS or **Help** in Windows operating system; and

2. click on the item **About Lightroom Classic... (figure 1.2)**.

Partial screenshot of Lightroom Classic software reprinted with permission from Adobe Systems Incorporated

1.2 - Lightroom Classic menu

The **About** window of the Lightroom software will appear (**figure 1.3**), where you can check the version of the software in use. In the case of this example, it is version **9.0**, as indicated by the red arrow. Note that the release may change due to new updates.

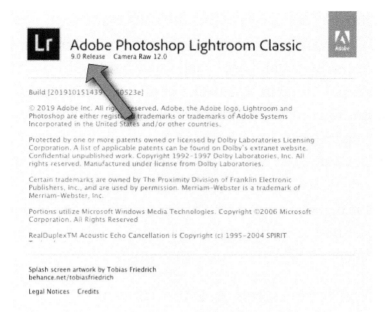

1.3 - About window and software version

The window is pretty much the same for both macOS and Windows versions of the software.

1.4 - Non-destructive Editing

An important feature of the Lightroom software is its **Non-destructive editing**. It means that no matter what changes you make to a photo, your original file will always be preserved. It makes it possible at any time to restart work from the beginning if the changes were unsatisfactory, or even from a certain point in the edit. It can be done with the **History** panel, to be presented in detail later in **Chapter 11 - Basic Photographs Editing**, located in **Volume #4** of the **Editing and Management of Photographs** series.

The Lightroom software records the edits made to maintain the integrity of the original files, as well as various photograph information, in its database called **Catalog**. In **Chapter 20 - Archiving**, located in **Volume #11** of the **Editing and Management of Photographs** series, the possibilities for preserving the work done in the software will be presented in detail. Basically, two of the options are manually export or copy the **Catalog**. Still, it is also possible to export the photographs with their metadata and edits made, incorporating them into the files generated in the export process, thus preserving all the work done.

1.5 - Lightroom Software End Products

At the end of a **Workflow** in the Lightroom software, the user will be ready to obtain one of the program's end products. The main one is exporting or sharing photographs in a highly compatible format, such as **JPEG** or **PNG**, for example. Another possibility is the direct publication on social networks. But you can also get other end products:

- ‣ **Map** - geographical view of the photographs;
- ‣ **Book** - complete and flexible book layout;
- ‣ **Slideshow** - creating a video with photo sequences;
- ‣ **Print** - creating layouts for printing; and
- ‣ **Web** - creating Web pages with the export of files in **HTML** format.

These options are in the upper right part of the **Workspace**, called **Module Selector**, to be presented later in **Chapter 3 - The Lightroom Software Workspace**. Photograph **Exporting and Sharing** will be covered in **Chapter 19 -**

Exporting and Sharing Photographs, located in **Volume #10** of the **Editing and Management of Photographs** series.

1.6 - Integration between Lightroom and Adobe Photoshop CC softwares

All the Adobe Creative Cloud online service software have tight integration with each other for data exchange due to the compatibility of your files and resources. However, in certain situations, it is necessary to perform some more specific tasks that the Lightroom software alone cannot solve. Having mastered the software and its many features will make it increasingly difficult to do so, but there are times when we want a feature that isn't available because it's not part of the software's reason for being.

If necessary, most of the time, the application that can solve the problem is the Adobe Photoshop CC software, which can be accessed directly from the Lightroom software itself, according to **procedure #02**.

Procedure # 02 - Editing Photography in the Adobe Photoshop CC Application from the Lightroom Software

1. select **Photo** menu;
2. click on the menu **Edit in**; and
3. click on the menu **Edit in Adobe Photoshop CC 2019...**

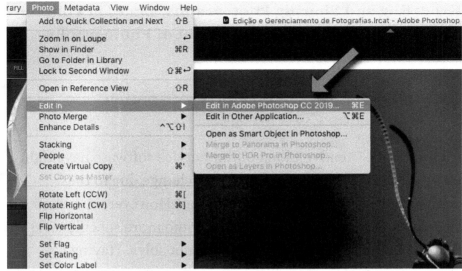

Partial screenshot of Lightroom Classic software reprinted with permission from Adobe Systems Incorporated

1.4 - Photograph editing in Adobe Photoshop CC software

As can be seen in **figure 1.4**, it is also possible to do advanced editing with other programs (note the **Edit in Other Application...** menu). But as previously mentioned, using the Adobe Photoshop CC software ensures more compatibility and better results because the software is produced by the same manufacturer (Adobe) and has as its high point the integration of applications of the Creative Cloud online service.

Note:

*In **item #3** of **procedure #02**, it may be that the version of the Adobe Photoshop CC application is different (in the case above CC 2019) since the Adobe software subscription system updates the version installed on the system from time to time. Therefore, your computer's menu version may not be CC 2019 at the time of reading this e-book. But don't worry, it doesn't affect the command at all.*

Also, if you are a professional or amateur photographer, you will probably want to purchase the **Photography** plan from the Creative Cloud online service, thus already having both programs that are part of the plan. Photograph editing in the Adobe Photoshop CC software is beyond the scope of this book.

Note:

*To edit photographs in another application, you need to access the Lightroom software preferences and set an additional external editor for the Adobe Photoshop CC software. If not previously defined, when the menu **Edit in Other Application...** is clicked the alert window of **figure 1.5** will be displayed. If desired, click the **Preferences...** button to specify the external editor.*

The Lightroom software **Preferences** window also allows for numerous other settings besides setting the external editor.

Partial screenshot of Lightroom Classic software reprinted with permission from Adobe Systems Incorporated
1.5 - Preferences button of the alert window about External Editor undefined

Clicking on the command button **Preferences...** opens a window with the same name, allowing you to choose the external editor by clicking the command button **Choose** (**figure 1.6**).

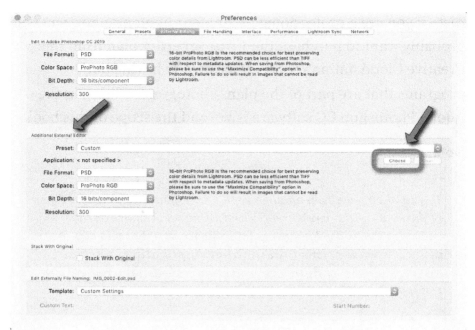

Partial screenshot of Lightroom Classic software reprinted with permission from Adobe Systems Incorporated

1.6 - Choose button from the Preferences window

Shortcuts

macOS	Windows	Action
Command + E	Ctrl + E	Edit photo in Photoshop software
Command + Option + E	Ctrl + Alt + E	Edit photo in another software

Review

Answer the questions below to consolidate the knowledge gained. The answers are in the **Appendix - Exercise Answers**.

1) What is the full name of the desktop version of the Lightroom software?

a) Adobe Lightroom
b) Lightroom Photograph
c) Adobe Photograph Lightroom
d) Adobe Photoshop Lightroom Classic
e) Lightroom System

2) What is the purpose of the Lightroom software?

a) Organize, manage, layer and edit images with specific features to organize and streamline the workflow of photographers, hobbyists and professionals alike, making them more productive
b) Digital photo editing and management with specific features to organize and streamline the workflow of photographers, hobbyists, and professionals alike, making them more productive
c) The organization, management, and editing of digital photographs with specific resources to organize and optimize the workflow of photographers, amateurs or professionals, making them more productive, with the possibility of inserting texts in images.
d) Only photo editing with specific features to organize and optimize the workflow of photographers, amateurs or professionals, making them more productive
e) Organizing, managing and editing video exclusively with specific features to organize and streamline the workflow of videographers, amateurs or professionals, making them more productive

3) Name two features commonly available in image editing applications that are NOT available in the Lightroom software?

a) Layer Usage and Text Input
b) Color correction and White Balance

c) Red-eye Correction and Local Adjustments
d) Use of Masks and Layers
e) Complex Cutting Tools and Selections

4) The Lightroom software was developed to cater to which type of user precisely?

a) Designer
b) Videomaker
c) Computer Technician
d) Engineer
e) Photographer

5) How can I get the Lightroom software?

a) Buying the DVD software from authorized distributors
b) Downloading the application from the Adobe company website on social networks
c) Through a subscription to the Adobe Creative Cloud online service
d) Accessing the Adobe Photoshop CC software site
e) Buying the software at newsstands

6) How are Lightroom software updates performed?

a) From the Adobe company pages on social networks
b) Automatically by the Creative Cloud online service application on your computer by clicking the Update button
c) By the Lightroom software website page
d) Lightroom software cannot be upgraded and new subscription required
e) Purchasing the DVD upgrade from an accredited vendor

7) How can you check the version of Lightroom software installed on your computer?

a) Making a phone call to Adobe and passing your copy serial number

b) In the Info window, accessed from the Lightroom> Lightroom Version (macOS) menu or the Help> Lightroom Version (Windows) menu

c) Accessing the Mode Selector and clicking Software Version

d) Accessing the Lightroom menu> About Adobe Photoshop Lightroom Classic... (macOS) or the Help menu> About Adobe Photoshop Lightroom Classic... (Windows)

e) Right-clicking the program icon in the Dock (macOS) or Taskbar (Windows) and accessing the Application Version link.

8) What is the Lightroom software feature that keeps the original photo files intact regardless of the edits made?

a) Advanced Edition

b) Conservative editing

c) Preservation incorporated

d) Non-destructive editing

e) Selective preservation

9) In addition to allowing the export or publication of edited photos on social networks, which of the end products below is NOT available in the Lightroom software Module Selector?

a) Book

b) Slide Show

c) DVD or Blu-ray recording

d) Print

e) Web

10) How can you edit a photograph in the Adobe Photoshop CC software from the Lightroom software using the application integration feature?

a) Opening the Adobe Photoshop CC software and editing the original photo file

b) From the menu Adobe Photoshop CC > Edit > Back to Lightroom

c) From the menu Photo > Edit In > Edit In Adobe Photoshop CC 2019...

d) Exporting the photo in the Lightroom software and opening it in the Adobe Photoshop CC software

e) From the menu File > Open in Adobe Photoshop CC > Edit

Important Notes:

Chapter 2

Differences Between Lightroom and Adobe Photoshop CC Software

Similar but for different purposes

The Lightroom and Adobe Photoshop CC software are mostly programs dedicated to photograph and image editing. They are capable of producing results that aim to meet the specific needs of its users, be they photographers, designers, digital artists, or those who produce photography and digital art as a hobby taken seriously.

In this chapter, we will examine their differences and commonalities, and present a comparative table to facilitate the identification of the application best suited to the execution of a given task.

Objectives of the chapter:

- ▸ know the capabilities of the Adobe Photoshop CC software;
- ▸ identify when to use the Lightroom or the Adobe Photoshop CC software; and
- ▸ determine when to use both software.

2.1 - Purpose of Adobe Photoshop CC Software

This e-book is not intended to address the Adobe Photoshop CC software, which is a complex application and considered by many, not to say the majority, to be the best for editing and composing photographs and images.

However, given that in certain situations the Lightroom software user may need the advanced features of the Adobe Photoshop CC software, the previous chapter discussed the integration between the two applications. Besides it, how it is possible, directly from the Lightroom software, to access the Adobe Photoshop CC software for sophisticated editing, complementing the work.

In terms of photo editing, the Adobe Photoshop CC software can do just about everything your younger brother, the Lightroom software, is capable of performing. With it, you can correct the tones of a photograph, its colors, its sharpness, reduce noise, edit only parts of the image, adjust the framing, use masks, and many other possibilities that are also present in the Lightroom software. But beyond all that, the Adobe Photoshop CC software also lets you:

- create complex compositions from two or more photos or images;
- use layers;
- include text;
- create shapes;
- apply sophisticated filters;
- use vectors;
- create complex selections; and
- many other unavailable possibilities in the Lightroom software.

Importantly, these features, which are missing from the Lightroom software, are not really an application deficiency. It was not designed to be image compositing software, such as the Adobe Photoshop CC application and other similar software on the market, such as we will see later.

The **figure 2.1**, located on the next page, is an example of a simple composition performed in the Adobe Photoshop CC software. Note the **Layers** on the right side of the screen surrounded by the red rectangle, where there is text (Sun Egret), shape (sun drawing, represented by a yellow circle), mask use, and more than one image in the same composition. The red arrows indicate some components of the image that could not be inserted into the Lightroom software.

Screenshot of Adobe Photoshop CC software reprinted with permission from Adobe Systems Incorporated

2.1 - Composition in the Adobe Photoshop CC software

In short, if the user's purpose is to edit photographs or images in a very sophisticated way or to create compositions with various images, text, shapes, and other resources for creating a graphic design or art, the most suitable is Adobe Photoshop CC software.

2.2 - When to use the Lightroom software

As you read the previous topic, the following question arises - if the Adobe Photoshop CC software is so powerful and has all the photo editing features of the Lightroom software virtually, why not just use it? The answer basically lies in managing large quantities of photographs and the productivity of editing tasks.

In the Adobe Photoshop CC software, photos are treated individually with typical commands **Open, Save, Save As..., Close**, etc. Besides, photograph editing tools are not directly arranged, and successive menus often need to be used unless several shortcut keys are stored (**figure 2.2**).

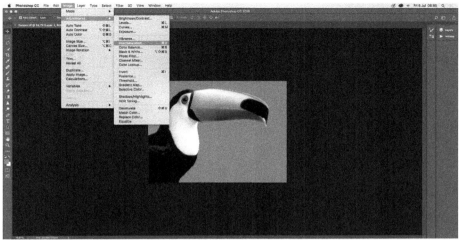

Screenshot of Adobe Photoshop CC software reprinted with permission from Adobe Systems Incorporated

2.2 - Successive menus in the Adobe Photoshop CC software

And they are not always available for all commands, although the software allows flexibility in its definition.

In the example above, you need to click **Image > Adjustments > Hue / Saturation...** to make this type of adjustment. Note that some commands have shortcut keys, some do not. Its interface, especially for the user who only wants to edit photographs, is initially challenging and takes a reasonable amount of time to reach the desired result. For this reason, the application requires a long learning curve.

Experienced users achieve higher productivity by using shortcut keys and using predefined actions, known as **Actions**. But even so, the application does not allow high productivity when the amount of photographs to be processed is too large as it is mostly not an image management application.

Another important feature for photographers is that the Adobe Photoshop CC software allows an image or photograph to be overwritten after saving changes, losing the original file. Although the program has some features to ensure a certain degree of preservation of these files, this is not a strict feature in the application as in the Lightroom software, whose **Non-destructive editing** prevents the user from modifying the original photo files with the edits made.

If you save a job in **PSD** format, native to the Adobe Photoshop CC software, it is possible under certain conditions and with some techniques of using layers to rewind and recover most or all of the original file. In the meantime, you can edit and save a photo over your source file and permanently change it.

Another feature of the software is its inherent inability to manage large amounts of photographs or images, making it difficult for tasks such as browsing, selecting, and searching. To get around it, there is a specific software for this purpose called Adobe® Bridge® (**figure 2.3**).

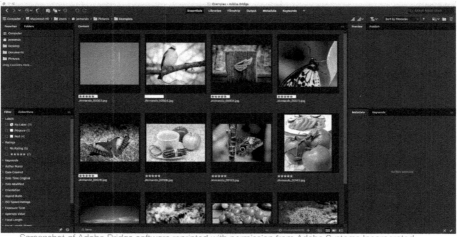

Screenshot of Adobe Bridge software reprinted with permission from Adobe Systems Incorporated

2.3 - Adobe Bridge software

The Adobe Bridge software lets you manage and classify large amounts of images, making them easy to catalog and search, and has many cool features. But it is a separate application, despite the possibility of being accessed directly from the menus of the Adobe Photoshop CC software.

All of these "limitations" of the Adobe Photoshop CC software are presented here to make it easier to understand the purpose of the Lightroom software. It specifically targets the user who doesn't want to create compositions and wants a tool for managing and editing photographs with a high degree of productivity. It is a common situation among professional and amateur photographers, especially those who have large amounts of images in their catalogs.

So, in short, the Lightroom software should be used when managing and editing many photographs efficiently and with high productivity, optimizing work time, and flow.

Note:

> *The Lightroom software also lets you manage videos and, with many limitations, perform some editing on this type of file. It is not, nor is it intended to be, a complete video editing program such as Adobe® Premier® Pro applications or Apple's Final Cut Pro® X.*

Ideally for the photographer is to use the Lightroom and Adobe Photoshop CC software together to benefit from both. The Lightroom software for productive photo management and editing, and the Adobe Photoshop CC software for more complex editing and composition. With these applications, the photographer will be equipped with the best and most sophisticated set of photographs management and editing applications. It's no coincidence that there is a plan called **Photography** on Adobe's Creative Cloud online service page, which makes both software available together.

2.3 - Lightroom and Adobe Photoshop CC Softwares Comparison Chart

The comparative table below is intended to consolidate the issues covered in this chapter by seeking to indicate which software is **best suited** for some of the key tasks involved in using it (**figure 2.4**).

Resource	Photoshop Software	Lightroom Software
Managing large quantities of photographs		X
Large quantity of photography editing		X
Composition of two or more images	X	Unavailable
Inclusion of text on images	X	Unavailable
Layer usage	X	Unavailable
Photograph Search		X
Sophisticated filters	X	Unavailable
Complex selections of areas in a photograph	X	
Nondestructive editing		X
High productivity in photograph editing		X

2.4 - Comparison chart between Adobe Photoshop CC and Lightroom software

Review

Answer the questions below to consolidate the knowledge gained. The answers are in the **Appendix - Exercise Answers**.

1) Which of these image editing tasks cannot be performed in Lightroom software?

a) Tone correction
b) Increased sharpness
c) Layer creation
d) Color corrections
e) Improvements in the framework

2) What is the name of the Adobe software that allows you to manage and catalog large quantities of photographs and has many other features that can be used in conjunction with the Adobe Photoshop CC software?

a) Adobe Illustrator
b) Final Cut Pro
c) Adobe Premiere
d) Adobe® Muse™
e) Adobe Bridge

3) Which of the following tasks can be performed directly in the Lightroom software?

a) Sharpness correction
b) Composition with two or more images
c) Inclusion of texts on photographs
d) Application of sophisticated filters
e) Complex selections in image areas

Important Notes:

Chapter 3

The Lightroom Software Workspace

Knowing the interface

In this chapter, we are going to cover the Lightroom software **Workspace**, presenting its main components.

Chapter objectives:

- ▸ identify the components of the interface;
- ▸ know the functions of each component; and
- ▸ know the Lightroom software **Modules**.

3.1 - Preferences Window

Before presenting the software interface, you have to know the **Preferences** window (**figure 3.1**). Here you can access several essential settings, such as the interface language.

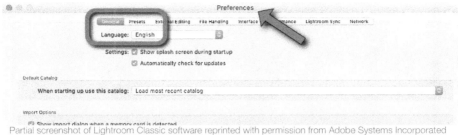

Partial screenshot of Lightroom Classic software reprinted with permission from Adobe Systems Incorporated

3.1 - Interface language option in the Preferences window

The options in the **Preferences** window will be detailed as needed throughout this book, as the possibilities abound. But I suggest that you scroll through the tabs at the top of the window, avoiding for the moment changing the settings.

The language preference can be changed in the **Language** drop-down list, highlighted in **figure 3.1**. To do this, follow **procedure #03**:

Procedure # 03
Change the language of the interface

1. open the **Preferences** window by clicking on the **Lightroom Classic > Preferences** (macOS) or **Edit > Preferences...** (Windows) menu;
2. on the **General** tab select the desired language from the **Language** drop-down list box;
3. close the **Preferences** window;
4. click on the **Lightroom Classic > Quit Lightroom Classic** menu; and
5. restart the Lightroom software.

After restarting, the software will display in the interface the language selected in **procedure #03**.

Another exciting setting of the **Preferences** window is the **External Editor** setting. It allows, directly from the Lightroom software, to edit and save a photograph, and then back to the application with the modifications made. This way, you can make more complex edits that could not be done in the software itself.

To configure the **External Editor**, click on the **External Editing** tab of the **Preferences** window. Note that if the Adobe Photoshop CC software is installed on your computer, the settings for external editing with this application will be available in the first section of the window, as shown in **figure 3.2**.

Partial screenshot of Lightroom Classic software reprinted with permission from Adobe Systems Incorporated

3.2 - Preferences window with External editing tab selected

Note that in the **Additional External Editor** section, the software to be used for external editing can be selected by clicking on the **Choose** command button located on the right part of the section and highlighted with a red arrow.

In the **Stack With Original** section, highlighted with a red rectangle, there is a checkbox with the same name as the section. It allows for stacking the photograph edited in the external program with the original image upon return to the Lightroom software. Photograph stacking will be covered in detail in **Chapter 10 - Viewing Filters**, located in **Volume #3** of the **Editing and Management of Photographs** series.

3.2 - Component Parts of the Workspace

The Lightroom software **Workspace** consists of nine main parts:

1. Identity Plate;
2. Module Picker;
3. Filter Bar;
4. Image Display Area;
5. Source Images Panel;
6. Metadata Panels, Quick Develop, and Configurations;
7. Local Adjustment Tools Strip;
8. Toolbar; and
9. Filmstrip.

The panels of items five and six in the above listing have their contents changed depending on the module selected in the **Module Picker (Library, Develop, Map**, etc.) The panels of item five are located on the left side of the **Workspace**, and item six on the right side. For the above listing, they are the **Library** module panels. Throughout the book, the panels will be presented depending on the module to be studied.

3.2.1 - Identity Plate

The **Identity Plate**, located in the upper left corner of the **Workspace**, allows you to customize the visual identification of the software on your computer screen and the progress of background activities such as photograph **Export**. Initially, it has the stylized letters "**Lr**," the software name and the username according to the data recorded in Adobe ID, as shown in **figure 3.3**.

Partial screenshot of Lightroom Classic software reprinted with permission from Adobe Systems Incorporated

3.3 - Identity Plate

You can customize the **Identity Plate** contents with **procedure # 04**.

Procedure # 04 - Custom Identity Plate

1. open the **Identity Plate Editor** window by clicking the **Lightroom Classic > Identity Plate Setup...** (macOS) or **Edit > Identity Plate Setup...** (Windows) menu;
2. after the **Identity Plate Editor** window opens, click the **Identity Plate** drop-down list box (**figure 3.4**);

Partial screenshot of Lightroom Classic software reprinted with permission from Adobe Systems Incorporated

3.4 - Identity Plate drop-down list

3. in the drop-down list box select one of the predefined options: **Adobe ID** for the display of stylized letters, software name and user logged in to Creative Cloud online service as in **figure 3.4**, or **Lightroom Classic** for the presentation of stylized letters only and the full name of the software;

4. in the same drop-down list box, select **Personalized** to enlarge the window and present **Identity Plate** customization options (**figure 3.5**);

Partial screenshot of Lightroom Classic software reprinted with permission from Adobe Systems Incorporated

3.5 - Custom option in the drop-down list Visual identity

5. if you want the Lightroom software to show background status and activities in the **Identity Plate**, leave the **Show Status and Activity** checkbox selected;

6. make the desired changes in the **Identity Plate Editor** window; and

7. click the **OK** command button to close the window and change the **Identity Plate**.

Customizing the **Identity Plate** allows you to enter user elements and tags using your own text or images, such as a logo by checking the **Use a graphical identity plate** option (**figure 3.6**). Also, you can choose the font for the **Module Picker**, located on the right side of the figure.

Partial screenshot of Lightroom Classic software reprinted with permission from Adobe Systems Incorporated

3.6 - Graphical and font choice for Identity Plate and Module Picker

Note:

*The **Show Status and Activity** checkbox allows you to display a progress bar when some background activity is in progress, such as when exporting photos (**figure 3.7**). I suggest keeping this checkbox enabled, as this will allow you to check the progress of your jobs quickly. You can continue to use the Lightroom software as usual while activities are in progress.*

Partial screenshot of Lightroom Classic software reprinted with permission from Adobe Systems Incorporated
3.7 - Progression bar during export of 251 background photos

3.2.2 - Module Picker

The **Module Picker** allows the user to change the tools and panels of the Lightroom software according to the tasks to be performed by the application. It consists of seven modules:

- ▸ Library;
- ▸ Develop;
- ▸ Map;
- ▸ Book;
- ▸ Slideshow;
- ▸ Print; and
- ▸ Web.

To select a module, click on its name in the selector. The software will automatically make modifications to the interface to make related panels and tools available. The currently selected module is in white letters, as in the example in **figure 3.8**.

toshop Lightroom Classic - Develop

Library | **Develop** | Map | Book | Slideshow | Print | Web

Histogram ▼

ISO 100   9.4 mm   f / 9,0   ¹/₅₀₀ sec

Original + Smart Preview

Basic

Tone Curve

Partial screenshot of Lightroom Classic software reprinted with permission from Adobe Systems Incorporated

3.8 - Module Picker

3.2.2.1 - Library Module

The **Library** module lets you manage source photographs, zoom in, browse their contents when zoomed (**Navigator** panel), manage photographs **Catalog** and storage **Folders**, **Collections**, use **Publish Services**, and **Import** and **Export** photographs. These functions are available in the left pane of the **Library** module, as shown in **figure 3.9**.

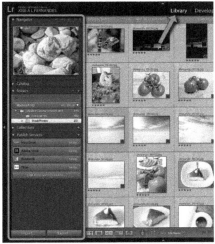

Partial screenshot of Lightroom Classic software reprinted with permission from Adobe Systems Incorporated

3.9 - The left panel of the Library module

In addition to these tasks, the module also allows you to perform other actions available in the right pane, such as **Histogram** view, **Quick Develop** (and limited), **Keywording**, **Metadata**, and **Comments** (**figure 3.10**).

3.10 - The right panel of the Library module

In the central part of the module, there is a large area where the photographs are displayed, originally in grid form. They come from one of the source panels located on the left side of the **Workspace**. This central part is called the **Image Display Area** and is present in most Lightroom software modules. In **figure 3.10**, you can see a part of this area, where the photographs are presented in miniature within the grid.

The **Library** module is best suited for viewing, searching, and locating the photographs in the **Catalog**.

3.2.2.2 - Develop Module

The **Develop** module's primary purpose is to edit the photographs, and all features are available to accomplish this task. It lets you navigate parts of a photo with the **Navigator** panel, zoom in, use **Presets**, manage **Snapshots**, access the editing's **History**, and use existing Collections, among many other possibilities.

Also, the **Copy...** and **Paste** command buttons, located at the bottom left, allow you to apply edits from one photograph to another, making the work more productive. These functions are available in the left pane of the **Develop** module, as shown in **figure 3.11**.

Partial screenshot of Lightroom Classic software reprinted with permission from Adobe Systems Incorporated

3.11 - Left Panels of the Develop Module

To edit photographs, the right side of the module provides panels for **Histogram** display, **Local Adjustments**, basic photo editing, and several other for more advanced editing, such as **Split Toning** and **Calibration**, for example (**figure 3.12**).

Partial screenshot of Lightroom Classic software reprinted with permission from Adobe Systems Incorporated

3.12 - Right panels of the Develop module

In the right panel are also the **Local Adjustment Tools**, which allow you to edit parts of the photograph using masks, unlike other panels whose edits affect the entire image. The **Local Adjustment** tools can be accessed through the **Local Adjustment Toolbar Strip** (**figure 3.12**). These tools will be covered in **Chapter 16 - Local Editings**, located in **Volume #8** of the **Editing and Management of Photographs** series.

The other modules of the Lightroom software called **Map**, **Book**, **Slideshow**, **Print**, and **Web** are primarily intended to do what their names suggest, that is, to display the photos in a

Catalog according to the output desired by the user.

3.2.3 - Filter Bar

The **Filter Bar**, located at the top of the **Library** module's **Image Display Area**, is intended to discriminate which photographs will be presented to the user based on some parameters. It is handy when we need to work on specific shots within an extensive **Catalog** with dozens, hundreds, or thousands of images. Besides, its use makes it much easier to search for photos, as we may restrict viewing to smaller sample size.

We can perform three types of filtering (**figure 3.13**):

- ▸ Text;
- ▸ Attribute; and
- ▸ Metadata.

Partial screenshot of Lightroom Classic software reprinted with permission from Adobe Systems Incorporated

3.13 - Filters available in the Filter Bar

Filtering will be presented in more detail in **Chapter 10 - Viewing Filters**, located in **Volume #3** of the **Editing and Management of Photograph** series.

3.2.4 - Image Display Area

In the **Image Display Area**, the user can view and search the photographs belonging to the **Catalog**, as well as access various other relevant information. They are arranged on a checkered canvas of customizable size. In each frame, there are icon-shaped buttons that allow you to perform multiple actions on one or more selected photographs. In **figure 3.14**, you can see some of these buttons and information mentioned below:

> ‣ flagging;
> ‣ rating star;
> ‣ add to the **Quick Collection**;
> ‣ rotate clockwise or counterclockwise; and
> ‣ color label.

Also, various other information can be viewed:

> ‣ filename;
> ‣ image type;
> ‣ file size;
> ‣ if the photograph has keywords;
> ‣ if the photograph belongs to any collection;
> ‣ if the photograph was cropped;
> ‣ if there was editing; and
> ‣ if the photograph has GPS coordinates.

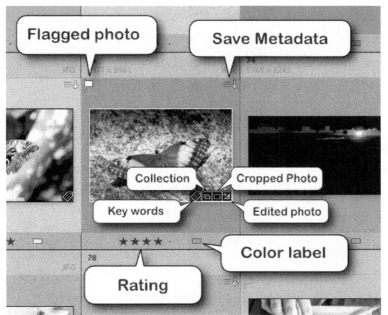

3.14 - Image Information in the Image Display Area

Figure 3.14 shows just some of the buttons and cited information that can be used or viewed in the **Library** module. To specify which of this information to display, you need to change specific **Image Display Area** settings that will be presented in this book as they are used. Other **Image Display Area** options are present on the **Toolbar** as shown below.

3.2.5 - Source Images Panel

The **Source Image Panel**, located on the left side of the **Workspace**, changes depending on the module selected in the **Module Selector**. It provides access to the location of photos with the **Catalog, Folders**, and **Collections** panels in the **Library** module, as well as other options such as the **Navigator** and **Publishing Services** panels. In the **Develop** module, they are modified to display the **Navigator, Presets, Snapshots, History,** and **Collections** panels. Observe in **figures 3.9** and **3.11** the composition of these panels for the **Library** and **Revelation** modules, respectively.

The vital thing in this chapter is to understand that the **Source Images Panel** allows access to the photographs in the **Catalog** for use by the various modules, always making available the **Collections** panel in all of them. Depending on the module selected, other panels may be available.

Specifically, in the **Library** module, it is also possible, from the **Source Images Panel**, to obtain information about the **Catalog** in use and to access the **Folders** in which **Collections** are organized. This subject will be further explored in **Chapter 7 - Importing and Organizing of Photographs**, located in **Volume #2** of the **Editing and Management of Photographs** series.

3.2.6 - Metadata Panels, Quick Develop, and other settings

These panels are located on the right side of the **Workspace** in the **Library** module, and allow you to set and change photographs metadata, perform quick and limited image editing, and enter keywords and comments. They can be seen in **figure 3.10** and will be covered in more detail in later chapters throughout the other volumes of the **Editing and Management of Photographs** series.

It is essential to keep in mind that, as with panels located on the left side of the **Workspace**, panels situated on the right side also change depending on the module selected in the **Module Selector**. It is suggested to go through the different modules to familiarize yourself with the various panels, even if you do not know what they do for now precisely. In the case of the **Revelation** module, for example, there are several panels for photo editing, as shown in **figure 3.12**.

3.2.7 - Expand and Collapse Panels

The Lightroom software panels can be expanded or collapsed to make the program more comfortable to use according to each user's preferences. To do this, click on the small triangle-shaped buttons or in their title bars. For the right side panels, the buttons are located on the right, as shown in **figure 3.15** for the **Library** module.

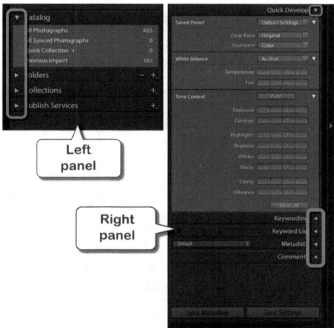

3.15 - Panel Expansion and Retract Buttons

Note that expanded panels have their buttons pointing down, and collapsed panels pointing left or right, depending on the side of the panel.

In addition to manually expanding and collapsing panels using their buttons, other beneficial configurations make it easier to organize the areas where they are located. The possibilities are:

▸ select which panels will be visible;
▸ show All;
▸ Solo mode;
▸ Expand All; and
▸ Collapse All.

In the specific case of the **Navigator** and **Preview** panels, the display options for the panels shown in the list above are nonexistent and can only be collapsed or expanded like the others. It is also not possible to disable them and their purpose is to allow the visualization of the photographs, and their details by zooming in or out, as can be seen in **figure 3.16**.

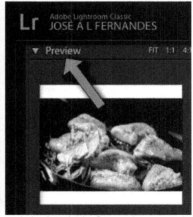

Partial screenshots of Lightroom Classic software reprinted with permission from Adobe Systems Incorporated

3.16 - Navigator and Preview Panels

These panels are fixed at the top left of the **Workspace**, above the others, and are present in all modules (**Library**, **Develop**, **Map**, etc.) Depending on the module selected in the **Module Selector**, it is called **Navigator** or **Preview**, but remains in the same position and has virtually the same features and functionality.

Except for the **Navigator** or **Preview** panels, to access visibility settings in all other panels, right-click the panel title bar, as shown in **figure 3.17**.

Partial screenshot of Lightroom Classic software reprinted with permission from Adobe Systems Incorporated

3.17 - Display panels options

Notice that the name of the clicked panel appears with an asterisk (*) beside it. Also, visible panels have a mark to the left of their names. In this example, only the **Publish Services** panel (indicated by the red arrow) is not visible. To make it visible, click its name in the list. If you want all panels to be visible, use the **Show All** option.

The **Solo Mode** option is handy. It allows only one panel to be open at a time. This way, with this option selected, whenever you expand one panel, all the others will collapse, freeing up space and making the area of the panels cleaner and more organized. Try clicking the triangular buttons and see how only one panel is expanded at a time if this option is selected.

To find out if the panels are in **Solo Mode**, look at the triangular buttons next to the panel names. When they are solid, it means that each panel can be expanded or retracted individually, as in **figure 3.17**. When dotted means that the panels are in **Solo Mode** mode, as shown in **figure 3.18**.

3.18 - Solo Mode of the panels

The other two options are **Expand All** and **Collapse All** (**figure 3.17**). They are self-explanatory and note that if **Expand All** is chosen, the **Solo Mode** will automatically be disabled if it is selected. The **Collapse All** option does not affect **Solo Mode**. Do the test to assimilate the operation.

For better organization of the left and right side regions of the **Workspace**, I prefer to keep the panels in **Solo Mode**, but this is a matter of personal choice.

3.2.8 - Local Adjustment Tools Strip

The photographs editing panels, located on the right side of the **Workspace**, allow corrections and adjustments that affect the entire photo. In the **Library** module, it is called the **Quick Develop** panel and has limited editing features. On the other hand, in the **Develop** module, there are numerous panels with all the editing features available. However, in these two modules, they allow general adjustments to the photograph. In many situations, only certain regions of an image need adjustment. For example, you may need to remove or soften a blemish on the skin, remove red-eye due to the use of the flash, or even a gradual tone correction in part of the photograph, such as a very bright or overexposed sky and land with good exposure, in the same picture. In such cases, corrections are not possible with typical editing panels as they would affect the entire photograph.

Local Adjustment Tools are an essential part of the Lightroom software, and they are located in the **Local Adjustment Tools Strip**, available exclusively in **Develop** module, as shown in figure **3.19**.

Partial screenshot of Lightroom Classic software reprinted with permission from Adobe Systems Incorporated

3.19 - Local Adjustment Tools strip

Its use is critical at more sophisticated levels of editing in the Lightroom software. It will be covered in depth in **Chapter 16 - Local Editings**, located in **Volume #8** of the **Editing and Management of Photograph** series.

3.2.9 - Toolbar

The **Toolbar**, situated at the **Workspace**'s bottom, has several functions and, like the panels, its configuration changed depending on the module being used in the Lightroom software. **Figure 3.20** presents the **Toolbar** for the **Library** module.

Partial screenshot of Lightroom Classic software reprinted with permission from Adobe Systems Incorporated

3.20 - Library module Toolbar

It quickly allows the user to change the way **Workspace** is viewed, copy keywords, and sort photos based on established criteria such as capture time or file name, among countless other possibilities, depending on the module selected.

Each module has its own specific **Toolbar**, and they will be addressed as needed throughout the volumes that make up the **Editing and Management of Photographs** series.

3.2.10 - Filmstrip

The **Filmstrip** allows you to quickly view and select photographs conveniently without having to change the display mode of the **Image Display Area** and the panels you are using.

It consists of photo thumbnails on a strip that allows you to scroll through all available images in the selected **Folder** or **Collection** and is located at the bottom of the Lightroom software **Workspace**. To bring a photo to the **Image Display Area**, click on its thumbnail. Photographs on the **Filmstrip** have frames with some information, such as those in the **Image Display Area** views (**figure 3.21**).

Partial screenshot of Lightroom Classic software reprinted with permission from Adobe Systems Incorporated

3.21 - Filmstrip

On several occasions throughout the volumes of the **Editing and Management of Photographs** series, the **Filmstrip** will be widely used to make the processes involved in photo editing and management more productive, thus facilitating the understanding of their capabilities.

Smart Tips!

Tip #1 - Saving the Visual Identity

If you have changed the **Visual Identity** of Lightroom software, be aware that you can save custom identities using the **Save As...** option in the **Identity Plate Editor** window, as shown in **figure 3.22**. That way, you can later easily switch between saved settings.

Partial screenshot of Lightroom Classic software reprinted with permission from Adobe Systems Incorporated

3.22 - Saving custom identities

Tip #2 - Quickly previewing a photograph

Mouse over without clicking on a photo in the **Filmstrip** and see it automatically enlarged in the **Navigator** or **Preview** panel, depending on the selected module, located in the upper left corner of the **Workspace**.

Tip #3 - Enlarging or reducing photo viewing

Use the **Thumbnails** slider, located at the far right of the **Toolbar**, to zoom in or out of photographs in the **Image Display Area** (**figure 3.23**).

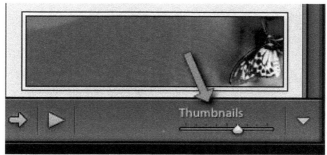

Partial screenshot of Lightroom Classic software reprinted with permission from Adobe Systems Incorporated

3.23 - Thumbnail slider

Shortcut keys

macOS	Windows	Action
Command + ,	Ctrl + ,	Open the Preferences window
\	\	Show / hide Filter Bar
G	G	Library Module
D	D	Develop Module
T	T	Show / hide Toolbar
Home	Home	Scroll Image Display Area to top
PageUp	PageUp	Scroll the Image Display Area one screen up
End	End	Scroll the Image Display Area screen to the end
PageDown	PageDown	Scroll the Image Display Area one screen down

Note:

*Using the shortcut key "\" to show or hide the **Filter Bar** only works this way in the **Library** module's **Grid View Mode**. In the other modules, it produces different results to be presented throughout the volumes of the **Editing and Management of Photographs** series.*

Review

Answer the questions below to consolidate the knowledge gained. The answers are in the **Appendix - Exercise Answers**.

1) Where can the user access the various settings of the Lightroom software, such as the language of the program interface?

a) Defaults panel
b) Preferences window
c) Import window
d) Historical panel
e) Adjustment Range

2) Which of the following is NOT part of the Lightroom software interface?

a) Toolbar
b) Film Strip
c) Filter Bar
d) Module Selector
e) Stamp Panel

3) In which part of the interface can you follow the progress of the activities being performed in the background?

a) Identity Plate
b) Source Images Panel
c) Image Display Area
d) Film Strip
e) Toolbar

4) Using the Module Selector, we can access the various features of the software. In which

module does the Lightroom software provide full photo editing capabilities?

a) Library
b) Develop
c) Map
d) Web
e) Adjustment

5) In which module are all features available for managing the Catalog's source photographs?

a) Database
b) Book
c) Print
d) Map
e) Library

6) Where are tools available for editing localized regions of photography using masks?

a) Adjustment Tools Panel
b) Title Bar
c) Punctual Editing Panel
d) Local Adjustment Tools Strip
e) Histogram panel

7) In which part of the Lightroom software workspace can we restrict the display of photographs based on specific parameters like Text, Attributes, and Metadata?

a) Selection panel
b) Import window
c) Filter Bar
d) Detail panel
e) Search panel

8) What is the name of the panel that is present in all modules of the Lightroom software?

a) Metadata
b) Adjustments
c) History
d) Edition
e) Collections

9) In addition to manually expanding and collapsing panels, other useful configurations make it easier to organize them in the areas where they are located. What is the name that allows you to view only one panel at a time, collapsing all the others automatically?

a) Show All
b) Collapse All
c) Solo Mode
d) Show Alternate
e) Expanded Mode

10) Which panels can only be collapsed or expanded without the other view configuration options available to other panels?

a) Navigator and Preview
b) Folders and Collections
c) Metadata and Import
d) Layout and Background
e) Snapshots and History

11) The Local Adjustment Tools Strip exists in which module only?

a) Library
b) Develop
c) Map

d) Book
e) Web

12) **Which part of the Lightroom software interface allows you to view and select photos conveniently quickly and without having to change the display mode of the Image Display Area and the panels you are using?**

a) Folders panel
b) Navigator Panel
c) Filmstrip
d) Excluded Range
e) Collections panel

13) **What is the slider's name located at the far right of the Toolbar used to zoom in or out of images in the Image Display Area??**

a) Thumbnails
b) Amplifier
c) Magnifying glass
d) Zoom
e) Scale

Important Notes:

Chapter 4

Photography Workflow

The Lightroom software in the photographic process

Using the Lightroom software is part of some stages of overall photographic production. Understanding your placement in the photographer's **Workflow** is critical to employing it to the best of your ability.

Chapter Objectives:

  ▸ present a **Workflow** proposal in Photography;
  ▸ position Lightroom software in the process; and
  ▸ allow an overview of the **Workflow**.

4.1 - Importance of the process

This book could have been written approaching the use of the Lightroom software, its menus, windows, panels, and all its components exclusively. But this approach would bring deficiencies that are difficult to remedy given flaws previously produced in other steps of the **Photography Workflow**. Some of these flaws can be circumvented in the application, and even eliminated, but not so much.

It is, therefore, critical that the photographer establishes a well-defined **Workflow**, minimizing these later difficulties, which will save him time when using the software in the **Post-production** phase. To achieve this goal, create a process to establish minimum standards of conduct in photographic activity, without limiting the creativity and work of the photographer.

There is no default process. Each photographer sets his own, which is being refined over time, and the experience gained mainly from mistakes that are often hard to forget. Thus, the purpose of this chapter is to present a **Photography Workflow** suggestion that will provide an initial starting point for those who have not yet developed it or refine existing ones. The most important thing is to recognize its importance and continually improve it.

4.2 - Phases of photographic production

In the following topics, the primary phases of a process proposal for the photographic activity will be detailed to define an efficient **Workflow** and the placement of the Lightroom software within that flow. As a suggestion, and based on my own experience, photographic activity can be divided into the following steps:

- Planning;
- Production;
- Post-production;
- Exporting, Printing and Sharing; and
- Archiving.

4.2.1 - Planning

Any human activity, regardless of its nature, will yield better results if a previous **Planning** is prepared in which the development of the actions to be conducted to achieve the expected goal can be anticipated. In photography, it is no different, especially when working professionally for a client, and one cannot make faults that are difficult to circumvent later. Imagine, for example, being hired to photograph a wedding ceremony and, at the famous "yes" time, find that the camera's battery is dead and that there are no spare batteries. If the job were to take pictures of a sunset in a particular location, it would be possible to go back and finish the task, even on another day, correcting the error without further consequences. It would be different from the day before, but it would still be a picture of the sundown at the place and time you chose. But how do you ask the newlyweds, the religious who conducted the event and the guests to redo a wedding ceremony the next day? Would it be possible to correct this planning flaw properly?

It is essential to point out that the **Planning** goes far beyond the charging of batteries and lens cleaning, through the detailed description of what, where, and how to shoot. The following are the main items from the **Planning** phase, based on my personal experience:

- Scheduling;
- A prior visit to the site of production;
- Script;
- Lens cleaning;
- Charging the batteries;
- Formatting of memory cards;
- Setting the camera's clock;
- Preparation of accessories;
- Confirmation of the date, time and place of the event; and
- Meteorology and other data from nature.

4.2.1.1 - Scheduling

The first thing to do is to schedule the appointment. It doesn't matter if it's on a paper calendar, computer, tablet, or smartphone. Be sure to record the day of photographic production. This way, you can plan ahead for the other steps in the Workflow. Besides, you avoid scheduling two events for the same day by compromising one of them.

In the case of electronic calendaring for computers and mobile devices, alarms can also be set to alert you to scheduled events in advance. It is very useful not to be surprised, which often leads to problems that are often difficult to solve in the nick of time. Get used to creating these alarms.

A good schedule allows you, when negotiating a job, to be sure whether or not you need to request a date change for the requested service if it is possible for the client. In some situations, it may even be impossible to do the service, given the immobility of certain events, such as weddings, graduations, birthday parties, etc. Showing an organization right now is a good sign for the customer.

If due to a **Scheduling** failure, already exists more than one event scheduled for the same day, it will be difficult to tell the grooms or college graduates three days before the scheduled date that you already have another undelayable appointment. Believe me, having a reliable schedule is critical to avoiding headaches and a lack of credibility in your services.

4.2.1.2 - Prior visit to the site of production

Often overlooked, this important step in planning can make work much easier. Knowing the way the conditions of the access roads and the traffic in advance can save the unpleasant situation of the photographer being late. In addition to indicating a lack of professionalism, this may make it impossible to capture essential photographs that would be produced early in the event, such as the arrival of guests, for example, in the case of social events.

Besides, with the **Prior visit**, you will be able to estimate a more accurate time to travel to the event location, taking into account, in addition to the distance and time to reach the destination. Also, the time needed to assemble the equipment and capture the previous photographs of the environments without people, in the case of social events. Even the difficulty of parking places, if relevant, are essential to avoid last-minute surprises. It prevents losing important photographs in the first moments due to stress, and the work will be done without unnecessary tensions that may compromise the photographer's concentration.

In addition to the issue of time, it is also essential to visit the venue well in advance to check technical aspects of photography, such as:

▸ on-site lighting conditions, such as intensity and the presence or absence of natural light, to define whether or not to use flash or other lighting equipment;

▸ the color temperature of the local lighting to attempt to set in advance, if possible, the White Balance on the camera;

▸ the color of the walls, the height and the color of the ceiling to evaluate the possibility of using the bounce flash;

▸ the best photo placements for critical events;

▸ checking the availability of places to obtain different angles, such as stairs, mezzanines, low floor parts, etc.;

▸ the best available scenarios and backgrounds for the photos;

▸ checking the availability of battery charging outlets and storage locations for accessories;

▸ in the case of social events, check the opening hours of the environment, such as a ballroom, for example, to allow the arrival time to be calculated in advance of the guests, and timely for the photographs of the room and decoration of the place, after prompt; and

▸ other information deemed pertinent according to the event or venue to be photographed. The more information you get, the easier the day job will be.

Importantly, the **Prior visit** to the workplace is not restricted to social events, but to any kind of photography, such as landscapes, animal life, outdoor rehearsals, etc. There are exceptions, such as still life photography (inanimate objects such as fruits, plates of food, objects, etc.), where objects are usually photographed in fully controlled environments and independent of strict times, thus dispensing with the **Prior visit**. There will be no surprises in these cases.

If the **Prior visit** is not possible, try to obtain as much information as possible from the client or the venue manager. In the case of ballrooms, event halls, theaters, etc., it is often possible to search the Internet for information about these venues and even to look at existing images of these environments, which helps a lot. This information will not replace the **Prior visit** in its entirety. However, it is better than arriving at the venue on the day of the event without any notion regarding the work environment.

4.2.1.3 - Script

I recommend that you define in advance what, how, and when to shoot on the day of production to avoid losing crucial moments, especially when photographing events that are often impossible to repeat. Besides, a good **Script** allows you to more precisely define work progress on the day, making it more predictable. The **Script** should also include the displacements with their estimated time to reach the event location, based on the previous step called **Prior visit**.

Try to make a written **Script** defining the framings, the light you want to use, the necessary preparations, the driving of the models if necessary, and the most appropriate time for the natural light you want to use, such as a sunset, for example.

There is no way to set a standard **Script** for all types of photography. Keep in mind that it is not intended to restrict work, as other opportunities usually arise for capturing good photographs. And the photographer should be prepared to enjoy them.

In the case of social events, try to talk to the people involved about what will be the dynamics of the event, who are the most important guests, what are the most emotional moments, how is the personality and age group of the protagonists of the event. Try to find out, for example, if they are formal, laid-back, children, elderly, etc. These data, added to those obtained during the **Prior visit** to the production site, already allow a good elaboration of the Script.

To give one more example, if you want to take a picture of a city, do some research on the most interesting places, learn a little about its history, how its residents live, their natural beauty, the most exciting times of the year, etc.

With this information, you will be able to establish more accurate scripts and make the most of the time to produce good photographs with the least clicks. And remember that in the case of distant landscapes and cities, for example, it is not always possible to have a **Prior visit** to the site, so it is essential to search in books, magazines and on the Internet. Tourism websites are a good start.

So, always make a **Script**! It will be your execution plan. If it's not too complicated and you don't want to write it down, do it at least mentally, but don't start the job without it. And try to elaborate it as early as possible to improve it over time. Often good ideas slowly emerge in your mind. Preferably write them down.

4.2.1.4 - Cleaning the lens

There are a few simple tasks that can save you a lot of time in **Post-production**. Lens cleaning is a typical case. After capturing two hundred photographs, you will find that in all of them there is always a blur or blurred dirt in the same position. And you didn't notice any of this when you were viewing the pictures on your camera's small **LCD** screen. Given the light conditions in place and the small size of these screens, even a well-trained eye may not realize the problem at the time of **Production**. Only after you import the photographs to your computer will you recognize the problem.

The good news is that the Lightroom software has useful features to fix it efficiently and productively on all your photos. But believe me, the software cannot work miracles, and the best way to deal with this problem is to avoid it. For all the power of Lightroom and Adobe Photoshop CC software, always keep in mind that attention to detail at **Production** can save you many hours later at your computer. With experience, you will quickly realize what will bring you future problems, and this is a skill that every photographer must develop over time. The best shot is one that needs the least hits in the **Post-production** phase.

So, avoid a lot of headaches and have a good lens cleaning before shooting, preferably the day before the event. There are numerous cleaning kits available on the market, and they are not usually expensive. Always have one of good quality because the return on investment is guaranteed.

4.2.1.5 - Charging the batteries

It seems obvious, but it is always worth remembering that without good and properly charged batteries, nothing can be done nowadays with digital cameras. Thinking about them is, therefore, a fundamental part of the process.

Professional and semi-professional cameras, usually **DSLR**, have long-life batteries if properly charged. Still, I always suggest having at least one spare and one charger to allow you to recharge at the venue while you are still working. It's unpleasant to interrupt work because of a low battery, and, believe me, it will always be missing at the worst time. So be prepared.

Note:

DSLR stands for Digital Single Lens Reflex, which is digital still cameras that use a mirror system to direct the light captured by the lens to the viewfinder located on the back of the camera where the photographer frames the scene. That is, what he sees is what is precisely framed by the lens, without deviations.

I suggest charging the batteries on the eve of **Production** and don't forget accessories that use batteries, such as flashes. It is possible to use ordinary batteries, but I recommend rechargeable batteries because they are more economical and allow recharging while working. Also, always try to use the same battery pack when recharging. For ease of identification, mark on the batteries by groups (e.g., I, II, III, etc.), with pens-type that write on the **CD** or **DVD** surface. Usually, they can also stick to the surface of the batteries. Therefore avoid mixing the battery packs to avoid charging the oldest and newest, which is not desirable.

4.2.1.6 - Formatting Memory Cards

The memory cards, where digital camera images are archived, have space limitations and require some care in the **Planning** phase. I always suggest **Formatting Memory Cards** before using them in new jobs. Especially if you take **RAW** photographs, which quickly take up large amounts of memory. This format stores all original information captured by the camera sensor without compression or processing.

Starting a new job without **Formatting Memory Cards** can become a severe issue at **Production** time, as during the event, it will be difficult to delete photos of old events without compromising service progress. You may notice that the memory card is full only after you have captured some images in the current event. That is, there may be old photos along with new photos on the same card. Consider deleting them without deleting the current ones if the memory card becomes full. If you format the card, you will lose the photos that have been captured so far in the current event. And erasing only old ones doesn't seem like a simple task, especially in the middle of a job. The chances are high that you will make irreparable mistakes in this situation.

To avoid this kind of problem, always have enough formatted cards for all the work, not forgetting the reservation cards. Preferably, avoid huge capacity cards in order not to lose all photos if any of them have problems. Today's most sophisticated cameras have two memory card slots, allowing you to increase the availability of photos to be captured. It is also possible to copy them all to the other card automatically by the camera itself, which ensures higher security against photographs loss in case of malfunction of one of the cards.

Note:

> *Preferably format the memory cards you will use in the camera itself. It ensures formatting compatibility with your equipment. Avoid formatting them on your computer as you may use other formats that may not be appropriately recognized by the camera. They all have a command in their menu that allows you to perform this task safely. Look for your location in your camera manual.*

4.2.1.7 - Setting the camera's clock

Little details observed in the **Planning** phase can make a big difference later. If you do not worry about Setting the camera's clock, your photographs may have incorrect dates and times in your **Metadata**, which is information that is automatically stored in files generated by digital cameras, and may be entered later, including in the Lightroom software. It may compromise future photo searches, among other issues.

Besides, the situation is aggravated by the use of more than one camera at the same event, a common procedure, especially in social events, sports coverage, and other cases in which there is a precise chronology.

If the **Setting the camera's clock** has not been previously performed, and one or more cameras have the wrong internal date and time, after importing the photographs to the computer, it will be possible to realize that they are out of chronological order. It happens due to the capture time in each will be different. In the case of a birthday party, for example, in a sequence of photos captured by a camera, children eating cake appear. Afterward, photographs from another camera appear with shoots of the "happy birthday to you." In case of a sporting event, pictures of the player celebrating that beautiful goal may appear and then images of the goal itself captured by another camera. We get the impression of being in front of a time machine.

The Lightroom software has the resources to fix this chronology issue by going to the **Metadata > Edit Capture Time...** menu, but it always takes time and has to be carefully done so as not to make the situation worse. Here it is still advisable to prepare beforehand to avoid wasting time later. The **Edit Capture Time...** command will be covered in **Chapter 10 - Viewing Filters**, located in **Volume #3** of the **Editing and Management of Photographs** series.

Finally, always check and set the date and time of all cameras using the configuration menus of each camera. By importing the photographs, they will be chronologically in order regardless of the number of cameras used without any further work later. Check the manuals for procedures for date and time settings.

4.2.1.8 - Preparation of accessories

Certain accessories are so necessary that they can make a big difference at the time of production. For sharp shots, for example, a tripod can be very valuable, as well as allowing aperture and camera speed settings that would not be possible without this accessory. A remote shutter is also very useful here, avoiding camera shake at the time of the shooting.

The examples above are just to remind you of the **Preparation of accessories** before you go out for a shot. It's no use remembering that the flash would be necessary at the moment of that picture of the university dean putting the graduation cap on the student's head if you left or forgot the flash at home or in the studio.

Which accessories that will be used will depend on what will be photographed, how, and where. So be sure to choose, separate, and prepare the essential accessories for your work in advance. Use the **Script** previously prepared to assist you in this task.

4.2.1.9 - Confirmation of date, time and place of the event

About three days before an event, confirm with the people involved and those responsible that the date, time, and place are confirmed. In addition to avoiding surprises, in the case of professional work, your clients will be happy to know that you are ensuring the smooth running of the services. And as a result, it will convey peace of mind, as they will usually be concerned with other details besides the photographs of the event.

Without intent or bad faith, compromises sometimes change, and if the person in charge fails, you may become unaware of the changes. Thus, the practice of confirming the **Date**, **Time**, and **Place** of events can save you from missing out on essential parts of your work, especially in the event of early hours, putting all the planning to waste. It also allows you to demonstrate professionalism to your customers and friends. The latter will often be your best advertisement.

4.2.1.10 - Meteorology and other data from nature

Depending on the type of work to be done, checking the weather and other data from nature is critical. If you want to photograph canyons, for example, it is good to check if it is going to rain and what the fog will be like, otherwise your trip and all your preparation may go downhill, or rather "downcanyon."

In **figure 4.1**, you can see a photograph with clouds covering a canyon, which would be the most exciting part of the image.

4.1 - A Photograph with a canyon covered in cloudiness due to weather conditions

The photograph as it is conveys a sense of mystery feeling due to the clouds, which is nonetheless impressive. Still, if your intention were a beautiful view of the canyon, then it would not be satisfactory. It would be necessary in this case to come back on another occasion with clear weather and a clear sky.

Want to photograph the northern lights? How about searching the Internet for sites that show the best predictions of places, dates, and time to view the beautiful phenomenon? How about seeing waterfalls at the peak of its river water flow?

That is, look for the best possible information about your topic to avoid the frustration of returning without any relevant results. Remember that even for photographs of social events, the weather should be taken into account as it can influence the external photos captured at the event and traffic, as you have to move to the venue where it will be held.

These days there are numerous websites on the Internet for any kind of weather forecast or natural phenomena. I prefer not to cite links, as they change constantly. I suggest that you do research citing the subject, and you will quickly have numerous relevant sites available. Prefer those with credibilities, such as universities, research centers, and government agency pages. Usually, they are more accurate and reliable.

4.2.2 - Production

If all were well planned in the previous phase called **Planning**, you would do your work as smoothly as possible without any unpleasant surprises. The **Production** phase involves everything that relates to the capture of the photographs themselves, from assembling and setting up the equipment on-site to, of course, the act of photographing, which is the most crucial part of the whole process.

Always remember to try to capture photos that require only minimal hits in the **Post-production** phase. In terms of image editing, good photography is one that requires little work at this stage. For example, it is much easier and faster to spend ten seconds taking that inconvenient plastic bag out of the frame before pressing the camera's shutter button, than to waste a lot more time after deleting it in **Post-production**.

Also, be aware of the exposure of the photograph. Overexposed or quite underexposed areas can cause loss of image information in the clipped areas, even using **RAW** format. In this case, not even the best image editing software can retrieve this information. To imagine that everything can be resolved in the **Post-production** phase is a mistake. Great photos can be lost due to small details.

4.2.3 - Post-production

After planning during the **Planning** phase and doing work in the **Production** phase, it is time for **Post-production**. This step does not only involve editing your beautiful photographs. Importing and selecting them correctly, among other activities, ensures more safety and productivity in your work.

The **Post-production** phase can be divided into the following steps:

- ▸ Backups;
- ▸ Importing;
- ▸ Selecting and Rating; and
- ▸ Editing.

It is in this phase of the **Workflow** that software for editing and management of photographs, such as the Lightroom software, are primarily used. The editing step can also be performed by applications that specialize in this task, such as the Adobe Photoshop CC software.

4.2.3.1 - Backups

After capturing your photographs, it is recommended not to start editing without first backing up your images. Please note that I spoke copies, ie, more than one. Without it, you could lose all your work. Worse yet, if it is a professional service for a customer, you will be in a quite awkward situation. Imagine having to inform him or her that all photographs of that extraordinary congress were regrettably lost.

In order to avoid this kind of problem, always keep in mind that doing safety copies of your photographs, well known as **Backup** in the technical vocabulary, is an indispensable part of the process. You may believe that while there is no logic to this, the more neglected this task, the higher the chance of a photograph loss problem, do not ask me why. You better not risk it.

The good news is, not surprisingly, the Lightroom software has the resources for this task. However, it is also essential to increase security with a few simple steps:

- ‣ avoid backing up only to your computer's hard drive. It will also store all original photographs for processing by the Lightroom software, and if you have a problem with this hard drive, there will be no backup to recover the images. Always try to use external hard drives;

- ‣ preferably, use two external hard drives for your backup, one that will always be connected to the computer and one to be stored in a different location, such as another room in your home or place of work, and disconnected from the computer. It may seem overkill, but it is easy to do and much better than running out of choice if necessary. In the event of an accident at your computer location, your photos will be preserved. Remember the famous popular saying that "who has one has none";

- ‣ if possible, back up in the event location where the photos were captured before returning to your place of business or residence using a laptop or portable card download accessory. It will already serve as one of the backups;

- ‣ if it was not possible to make the copies at the event location, before opening the Lightroom software, or any other photograph editing program, make a copy of the photos on the memory card to at least one external hard drive;

- ‣ use the **Make a Second Copy To** option of the **Import** window of the Lightroom software when importing photos from the memory card and select an external hard drive for the copy generation that is always connected to the computer. This subject will be presented in more detail in **Chapter 7 - Importing and Organizing of Photographs,** located in **Volume #2** of the **Editing and Management of Photographs** series;

▸ another option is to archive your original photographs on optical media such as **CD, DVD,** and **Blu-ray** discs. It is important to select the **Verify Copy** option in the recording program so that it is verified at the end of the process that the recording is perfect. And before storing the discs, make tests to confirm that the files can even be accessed by the media player;

Note:

*Depending on the program, the copy verification option may have other names, such as "**Test Copy**," for example. Check the manual of your CD, DVD, or Blu-ray burning software for more information.*

▸ if the photograph editing software you are using has the option to **Move** photos, avoid using them. While moving files from the memory card to the computer's hard drive, problems may occur, and they may become corrupted. Always prefer the **Copy** option; and

▸ avoid formatting the memory card immediately after copying the photos to the computer and backup hard drives, as there is no need. Only format memory cards when doing another job, as mentioned in the **Planning** phase. That way, your files will still be there in case of any eventuality.

These **Workflow** proposals for doing **Backups** are just suggestions, and each photographer has their way of accomplishing the task and the level of security considered sufficient for each case. However, it is unquestionably the need to make some kind of copy before starting any work.

Following the suggestions given, I believe you will hardly have problems with losing your photographs. Remember that in these times of digital photography, it is effortless to delete or lose files permanently. Therefore, I recommend never neglecting your copies as it is quick and elementary to make them. However, it is tough and painful to recover lost photographs.

This is difficult to happen, but problems may occur with the **Catalog** you are working on. Recovering a corrupted or misusing Lightroom software **Catalog** will be presented in **Chapter 20 - Archiving**, located in **Volume #11** of the **Editing and Management of Photographs** series.

4.2.3.2 - Importing

Once you've backed up, it's time to bring your photos into the Lightroom software, and this process is called **Importation**. It is a crucial step, with several possibilities beyond merely copying the images into the software **Catalog**.

Once imported, the photographs will be ready for selection, sorting, filtering, and editing. A well-conducted **Importation** facilitates and makes the other steps of the **Lightroom Software Workflow** more productive. Therefore, it is important to know your resources well. The photo **Importing** phase will be covered in detail in **Chapter 7 - Importing and Organizing of Photographs**, located in **Volume #2** of the **Editing and Management of Photographs** series.

4.2.3.3 - Selecting and Rating

Every photographer, amateur or professional, knows that not all captured photographs are usable and that it is often necessary to make choices between several options of the same photograph or to eliminate those considered useless. The **Selecting and Rating** phase, therefore, aims to define which photos will be edited and to rating them in scales of importance, according to their quality and user's taste. The Lightroom software has many tools that allow image rejection, flagging, and rating, as well as filters that will enable the user to view specific groups of photos according to previously established search criteria. These are essential features for photographs management and will be covered in **Chapters 8 - Photographs Viewing Modes**, **9 - Photographs Marking and Selecting**, and **10 - Viewing Filters**, located in **Volume #3** of the **Editing and Management of Photographs** series.

4.2.3.4 - Editing

After importing, selecting, and sorting phases, it is time to edit the photographs. **Editing** involves many tasks, such as:

- ▸ cutting and framing;
- ▸ white balance corrections;
- ▸ corrections in exposure, contrast, and saturation;
- ▸ color adjustments;
- ▸ sharpness corrections and noise reduction;
- ▸ hits in perspective;
- ▸ exclusion of unwanted stains and details;
- ▸ making local adjustments; and
- ▸ other specific corrections such as red-eye reduction.

In addition to the above editings, many more are available in the Lightroom software for photograph enhancement. And by utilizing the ability to edit them in the Adobe Photoshop CC software directly from the Lightroom software, returning to it at the end of editing, the possibilities are greatly enhanced by access to a multitude of features, limited only by the user's creativity. However, most edits can only be done with the Lightroom software, whose **Workflow** is far more productive for processing large numbers of photos quickly without the advanced features of the Adobe Photoshop CC software.

Photograph editing will be covered in detail in **Chapter 11 - Basic Photographs Editing**, located in **Volume #4** of the **Editing and Management of Photographs** series. Other chapters and volumes in the series will introduce more advanced techniques, such as color correction and sharpening and noise enhancement.

4.2.4 - Exporting, Printing and Sharing

In any process, there are basically the steps known as **Input**, **Processing**, and **Output**. In our process of using the Lightroom software, we input our photographs in the **Import** phase, process them in the **Editing** phase, and finally produce the output in the **Exporting, Printing and Sharing** phase. In the end, all work is aimed at this phase of the process. The end product we want is selected photographs, edited, and ultimately exported, printed or shared with others.

Export means creating new files with edits made, and metadata entered or changed. Due to the non-destructive feature of the

Lightroom software, these new files will not be the same originals we imported from the camera's memory card. These are other files generated in different formats, according to the user's choices. On export, the Lightroom software offers several configuration possibilities, such as:

> - **JPEG, PSD, TIFF, PNG, DNG**, and **Original** image format;
> - picture quality according to its compression level;
> - color space embedded in the photograph;
> - inclusion of watermark; and
> - renaming of the files.

It's important to mention that the Lightroom software itself already has ready-to-export settings for specific-purpose photos, known as **Presets**, such as exporting to email programs that require smaller photos for transmission over the Internet. It is also possible for the user to create and save their own settings for later use. **Presets** will be presented in **Chapter 15 - Presets**, located in **Volume #7** of the **Editing and Management of Photographs** series.

Besides **Exporting**, another possibilities are the **Printing** and **Sharing** of photos. It is possible to publish directly on social networks, which significantly facilitates your posting. In this case, instead of generating files on your computer's hard drive, you will be prompted to log in to the sharing service, and the Lightroom software itself will post. **Exporting** and **Sharing** Photographs will be covered in more detail in **Chapter 19 - Exporting and Sharing of Photographs**, located in **Volume #10** of the **Editing and Management of Photographs** series.

4.2.5 - Archiving

In the final phase of **Photographic Workflow**, it is vital to take steps to preserve the work done in the editing application, which in the case of this book, is the Lightroom software. You can do this by exporting the entire **Catalog** to an external storage unit, permanently and definitely. But there are other possibilities, and the various **Backups** created to preserve the originals should not be forgotten. At this stage, they should be analyzed for your needs according to the desired security level and available storage space.

Keep in mind that the original files from the camera are the modern version of the old reel film. As at that time, it is crucial to keep at least one copy of your originals for future needs, as you may need to "reveal" your files again and differently. The archiving copy of the originals should be stored in the same location as the Lightroom software **Catalog** so that it is easier to locate and reopen in the future if necessary.

In the Lightroom software, you can work with only one **Catalog** to manage all photographs of multiple projects. However, other approaches are possible, such as creating specific catalogs for certain jobs or periods, at the user's discretion. Each way to create and manage catalogs has its advantages and disadvantages, including archiving, and the best approach depends mostly on the specific needs of the user. Archiving photographs and Lightroom software catalogs will be covered in detail in **Chapter 20 - Archiving**, located in **Volume #11** of the **Editing and Management of Photographs** series.

4.3 - Photography Workflow Overview

The flowchart below presents the main steps of the proposed workflow to provide an overview of the process (**figure 4.2.**)

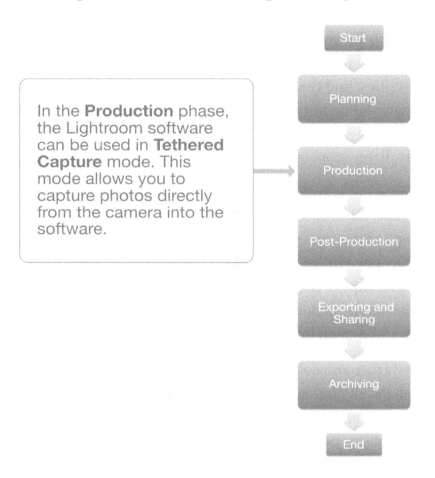

4.2 - Photography Workflow

Smart Tips!

Tip #4 - Kids Party Accessory

To get the kids' attention, buy straps-themed for the camera, or attach colorful stickers you already own. It will be easier to capture the attention of the little ones and thus get good pictures with broad smiles.

Tip #5 - Memory Cards #1

At the end of an event, take the memory cards out of the camera and put them in an appropriate package, storing them in your pocket. If the equipment is lost or stolen, you will not lose the photographs. A very appropriate tip when shooting events for clients. You will have equipment damage, but at least you will not lose the customer payment and have no significant problems with it. If the camera allows you to use two cards, use the option to copy photos to the second card automatically. At the end of the event, I suggest keeping one in your pocket. Leave the other in the camera.

Tip #6 - Memory Cards #2

Your card has problems and does not allow reading of the photos? Before you despair, go to the card manufacturer's website and check the availability for downloading a data recovery program on damaged cards. Usually, you should find it, but if you can't, try to find a similar program at the online software stores.

Tip #7 - Preview with the Camera

During the **Prior Visit**, take the camera and study the lighting and equipment settings for proper exposure. Do tests. Then save these custom settings if the camera has this option, which is usually available in the camera menu, or write down the aperture, speed, and **ISO** sensitivity parameters. On the day of the event, if conditions do not change, use the same saved settings normally accessible by **U** mode on the camera's mode dial. It is interesting to make the **Prior Visit** at the same time as the event to obtain similar lighting conditions. Any changes may be corrected with minor adjustments, as you will have already made the main settings beforehand.

Tip #8 - Cleaning the lens during production

As already mentioned in this chapter, cleaning camera lenses is an essential activity during the **Planning** phase. Still, always shoot with an appropriate flannel in your pocket for lens cleaning. If it happens to get dirty, you don't have to be taking pictures with persistent stains. It's not difficult, for example, to put your finger on the lens and create a blur that is hard to see when viewing photos on your camera's small **LCD** screen. But it sure will appear when you edit the images later. Believe me - a small, seemingly irrelevant flannel in your pocket can save you a lot of work later.

Tip #9 - Ultraviolet Filter

The lens is an expensive accessory, especially those of good quality and wide maximum aperture with small **f-number**. Therefore, always have an ultraviolet (**UV**) filter in front of the lens. In addition to filtering out **UV** rays, you protect the lens from impact. The filter's cost is negligible near the loss of any lens breakage. If you need to take it off to obtain the maximum sharpness, take the pictures and put them back in. In typical situations, the **UV** filter does not change much the sharpness.

Review

Answer the questions below to consolidate the knowledge gained. The answers are in the **Appendix - Exercise Answers**.

1) What are the phases of Photography Workflow suggested by the author of this eBook?

a) Preparation, Production, Export, and Sharing
b) Production, Post-production, Archiving, and Distribution
c) Installation, Editing, Archiving, Sharing, and Printing
d) Planning, Production, Post-production, Export and Sharing, and Archiving
e) Archiving, Production, Printing and Post-production

2) At what stage of the planning are the lighting conditions of the place and the possible positions for good photographs evaluated?

a) Photographic Analysis
b) Prior Visit
c) Post-production
d) Importation
e) Production

3) The dynamics of a photographic work should be studied and detailed at what stage of the Planning phase?

a) Search
b) Lens cleaning
c) Sharing
d) Selection and Classification
e) Script

4) Which stage of the planning aims to avoid persistent spots or dots in the captured photographs?

a) Search
b) Lens cleaning
c) Scheduling
d) Battery charge
e) Archiving

5) At which stage of the planning do you try to ensure that the photographs of all cameras used in work will be in chronological order after being imported?

a) Prior visit
b) Reconfiguration of machines
c) Battery test
d) Scheduling
e) Clock setting

6) At what stage of the Photography Workflow does the photographer capture the images?

a) Planning
b) Production
c) Post-production
d) Export and Sharing
e) Archiving

7) What should you do before doing any work with the original photographs?

a) Backups
b) Non-destructive editing
c) Formatting of memory cards
d) Select the best images
e) Rate the photos

8) Which of the following does NOT provide good security for storing copies of original photographs?

a) On the external hard drive connected to the computer

b) On laptop at the production site

c) On the same hard drive where the Lightroom software is installed

d) On optical media such as DVD and Blu-ray

e) On the external hard drive that is stored in another room

9) What should you do after importing the photographs?

a) Selection and Rating

b) Image Editing

c) Clock Setting

d) Image Analysis

e) Export

10) Which of the tasks below is NOT performed in the Editing phase during the Post-production phase?

a) Color correction

b) Sharpness adjustments

c) Photograph sharing

d) Correction in perspective

e) Elimination of stains

11) At which stages of the Workflow is the Lightroom software most used?

a) Post-production, Exporting, and Sharing

b) Planning, Production and Post-production

c) Production, Post-production, and Sharing

d) Planning, Production and Archiving

e) Post-production, Sharing and Distribution

12) What is the main purpose of the Archiving phase?

a) Copy the original photos to a safe place
b) Store memory cards with original photos
c) Store and preserve photographic equipment after use
d) Preserve the work done in the editing program
e) Archive files with JPEG extension

13) What is Tethered Capture mode, and at what stage we can use the Lightroom software with it in the Photography Workflow?

a) Timer photo capture by the Lightroom software. Production phase.
b) Capture photos directly from the camera to the Lightroom software. Production phase.
c) Capture photos by the Lightroom software import module. Post-production phase.
d) Video capture by the linking module of the Lightroom software. Import phase.
e) Transfer captured images via wifi to the Lightroom software. Planning phase.

Important Notes:

Chapter 5

Image File Formats

Knowing the purposes and differences

A photograph produced by a digital still camera, be it a compact camera, a smartphone, or a professional, will be recorded in a digital file that will later be transferred to a computer, edited, archived, printed, and exported or shared.

Typically cameras produce **JPEG** digital files that are small in size and highly compatible with many devices. However, the most sophisticated models also offer the **RAW** format that stores all photo information captured by the camera sensor. This format has many advantages at the time of editing but generates much larger files, and their compatibility is low.

In addition to **JPEG** and **RAW**, there are other image file formats available for specific purposes. Knowing the key is critical for photography professionals and lovers, as well as those who perform image editing tasks.

Objectives of the chapter:

▸ know the main types of image files;
▸ deciding when to use **RAW** format on the camera;
▸ deciding when to use **JPEG** format in the camera; and
▸ compare **RAW** and **JPEG** formats.

5.1 - Main types of image files

There are numerous image file formats for digital photo storage. Each has specific characteristics and purposes. The most common are:

▸ JPEG;
▸ RAW;
▸ DNG;
▸ PSD;
▸ TIFF;
▸ PNG ; and
▸ GIF.

5.1.1 - JPEG Format

JPEG stands for *Joint Photographic Experts Group*. It is a very popular file format that uses data compression to generate small files and is widely used in digital photography and imaging devices.

A **JPEG** file can use the extensions "**.jpg**" or "**.jpeg**," and usually both are supported by image editing programs and computer operating systems. **JPEG** allows variable rates of lossy data compression, which directly affects image quality and final file size. Higher compressions reduce file size but decrease image quality. **Figure 5.1** shows the same image exported in two **JPEG** files with different compressions and, therefore, different final qualities.

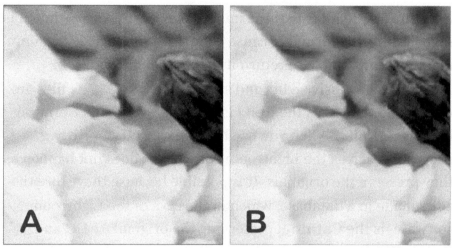

5.1 - Same photograph exported in JPEG format with different compressions

The images in **figure 5.1** have been enlarged by **190%**, to make the differences more comfortable to see, showing only a small part of the photograph. Image "**A**" was exported in the Lightroom software with **10%** compression (low), and image "**B**" with **90%** compression (high). The final file size of "**A**" is **9.3 Mbytes** (9,300 KBytes) and "**B**" **465 Kbytes**. That is, it is twenty times smaller than the "**A**." This drastic reduction in file size comes at a price. Note that comparing images (**A** and **B**), the image quality "**B**" is reduced, especially in the contour details and graininess. However, depending on the purpose, the image may be acceptable.

In high definition photographs, this loss of quality is a big problem. However, if the goal is to reduce the file, **JPEG** allows a lot of flexibility in the quality ratio. Test when exporting a file to get a proper relationship between these two factors, according to the ultimate purpose of the photograph.

A significant detail is that the image loses quality every time it is saved in this file format because compression is applied again, making it impossible to return it to its original condition. Therefore, successive edits and saves directly to **JPEG** files are not recommended as the trend is for progressive deterioration in image quality. When you use **Nondestructive editing** programs such as the Lightroom software, it does not happen as they preserve the originals. It is possible because they store the edits made in a database, which in the case of the Lightroom software, is the **Catalog**, preserving the original **JPEG** and maintaining its quality. Each time the photo is reopened in the software or exported, it reapplies all edits to the original file and creates a new view, preserving it all the time.

JPEG is a highly compatible format between operating systems and image editing programs, allowing easy sharing between computers and the Internet. The vast majority of digital cameras, and various image capture devices such as scanners, generate **JPEG** files from the raw data captured by your sensor.

Depending on the camera, the photographer may have some control over the conversion to **JPEG** format of data captured by the camera's sensor, setting parameters for this task. In the case of the Nikon D7100, this feature is called **Picture Control**. Once one of your options is selected, the sensor data will be converted ("revealed"), taking these adjustments into account. For example, if you want to "reveal" in black and white, select **Monochrome**, and the **JPEG** will be a grayscale image taken from the data captured by the camera sensor. To shoot portraits, choose **Portrait**, which will allow you to produce a smoother, shallow depth of field image. Look in your camera's manual for how to use this feature if available, and test with the various options. See also **Smart Tip #15 - Enhancing Camera Development** at the end of this chapter for more information.

JPEG does not support transparencies. If you need the final image to have areas with this feature, you will need to choose other formats.

5.1.2 - RAW Format

The **RAW** format is named this way because, in reality, it is a data file containing all the information captured by the camera's sensor, with no changes or compressions. And this information is recorded in different manners, depending on the camera manufacturer. This data needs to be "revealed" by an application to become a visible image, which in Adobe's case is **Adobe Camera RAW**. It contains the instructions necessary to read this type of file from different manufacturers.

The Lightroom software can natively open **RAW** files and doesn't need another application for this, which is a great advantage. In the case of the Adobe Photoshop CC software, for example, **Adobe Camera RAW** is previously opened for the **RAW** file to be "revealed" before the image is available.

Not all cameras offer the ability to capture images in this format, usually restricted to semi-professional and professional models. Smartphone and compact cameras typically do not have this capability, delivering the photograph to the user in **JPEG** and ready to view or share.

Note:

*Currently, some manufacturers of compact cameras and smartphones are starting to offer the possibility of generating files in **RAW** format.*

When importing a **RAW** file into the Lightroom software, it automatically recognizes the file as if it were of any other format, and includes it in your **Catalog**, as this capability is native to the program.

RAW format is considered the "digital negative" of current still cameras. It does not perform data compression and therefore generates much larger files, quickly taking up a significant amount of space on your computer's memory card and hard disk.

Look at **figure 5.2** for the same original photograph captured in **RAW** and **JPEG** formats, the latter with the lowest compression possible to produce the best final image quality. Neither file was edited after capture, and **JPEG** was processed only on the camera itself.

5.2 - Photograph captured simultaneously in JPEG and RAW

The left photograph (**A**) is in JPEG format. Its file has a size of 20.7 Mb. The right one (**B**) is in **RAW** format, and its file is 31.9 Mb. That is, the figure "**A**" is about 1/3 smaller than the "**B**." A considerable reduction, even keeping the highest quality **JPEG** in the camera. Changes in exposure and other details in the final **JPEG** image are due to the camera's developing settings.

If you have the option to shoot both **RAW** and **JPEG** simultaneously on your camera, try capturing photos in both formats, varying the **JPEG** quality and camera development settings, and then comparing the size, quality, and image changes of the two files. With my camera, using the lowest quality **JPEG** (highest compression), any picture used as an example was the size of 5.1 Mb, and the **RAW** of the same image with 31.7 Mb. In this case, **JPEG** it's about six times smaller than **RAW**. Full compression and final image quality will also depend on details such as the presence or absence of large amounts of continuous color areas that can make the file even smaller.

Each camera manufacturer creates its **RAW** file format by adopting its filename extension, such as ".**NEF**" on Nikon® and ".**CR2**" on Canon®. These proprietary formats cannot be opened in any image editing program except those from the manufacturer itself or through other computer programs such as Lightroom and Adobe Camera RAW softwares, which already can read these files from various manufacturers internally. Manufacturers themselves often make applications available with their cameras that allow them to open and edit these proprietary formats of their **RAW** files. The drawback is that these formats can be changed or even replaced, creating problems in the future for their reading and interpretation.

Despite these limitations, the **RAW** file has advantages for the photographer, especially professionals, since all the information captured by the camera sensor is available for later editing of the photograph. This way, it has much more flexibility at the time of editing, and it is possible to retrieve more information from light, dark, and shadow areas than in **JPEG** files. It happens because much of this information would have been discarded by compression, which considerably limits the range of corrections.

Another great advantage of the **RAW** format is the ability to change the **White Balance (WB)** at the time of editing, which frees the photographer from one more concern during the **Production** phase, ie, when capturing photographs. Although it is interesting to set this setting right now, this is not always easy, especially when the lighting conditions of the venue change frequently. With **RAW** capture, this problem is much easier to solve when editing, because the camera will not have previously applied the adjustment as it does in **JPEG**, which is not always the best result.

You can change **White Balance** with any other image file format supported by the Lightroom software, but in the case of **RAW** files, this adjustment is much more flexible and accurate, as can be seen from the numerous options available in the example in **figure 5.3**.

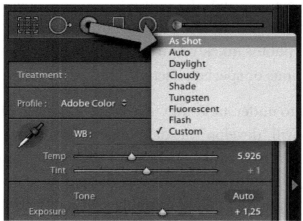

Partial screenshot of Lightroom Classic software reprinted with permission from Adobe Systems Incorporated

5.3 - White Balance (WB) drop-down list options from a RAW file

The **White Balance** options in **figure 5.3** are from the **RAW** file of the photograph in **figure 5.2** (**B**). In the case of photograph "**A**" in **JPEG** format, the options are much narrower, as shown in **figure 5.4**.

Partial screenshot of Lightroom Classic software reprinted with permission from Adobe Systems Incorporated

5.4 - White Balance (WB) drop-down list options from a JPEG file

Thus shooting in **RAW** will give you more flexibility in **Post-production** to make more accurate **WB** corrections than in **JPEG**. In short, the photographer has much more possibilities for editing and artistic creation in a **RAW** image than in **JPEG**, hence the preference for capturing in this format whenever possible. It is evident that **JPEG** also has its advantages, for example: in situations where memory card space is low, if you need to move photos quickly or if you want to edit them without major corrections or special effects.

It is essential to understand that in a **JPEG** captured photo, the camera itself will "develop" the data obtained by the sensor (**figure 5.5**). Thus, it applies **White Balance**, compensates for exposure, adjusts saturation, contrast, sharpness, and various other adjustments, and may even apply special effects if the camera has these features.

However, once this "revelation" happens, if you need to edit the photograph, it will be done in this **JPEG** file previously processed by the camera. It will not always be entirely your way, and you will not be able to return to the original data captured by the camera sensor for greater editing flexibility.

Always keep in mind that no matter how good your camera is, the power and flexibility of editing a **RAW** file in Lightroom or **Camera RAW** software is far higher than that automatically done by the camera. So whenever possible, shoot in this format.

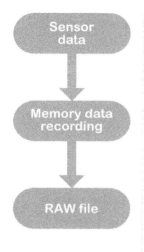

The left-side workflow shows what happens with the sensor's data for archiving using the RAW format in the memory card. Look how the data are recorded and the way they left the sensor, without any development or compression. The right-side workflow shows the sequence actions done by the camera when we shoot in JPEG format. In the red balloons happen the phases of development and compression of data. Even though the camera usually does a good job, it can know exactly neither the photographer's intention nor if the corrections will be the expected. It is possible, in many cases, that it even does in the wrong way. The JPEG file is more practical, but if the photographer doesn't enjoy the development of the photograph, there won't be so much flexibility for the adjustments, like in the case of the RAW file.

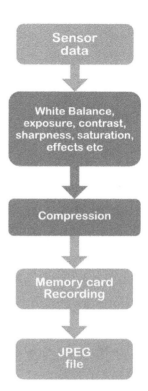

5.5 - RAW and JPEG processing

5.1.3 - DNG Format

DNG stands for **Digital Negative,** and this is the idea of this file format created by Adobe to establish a standard that is non-existent in **RAW**, in which each manufacturer defines its proprietary format. The extension of a **DNG** file is its name (**.dng**), and, like the **RAW** format, it stores all information captured by the camera sensor.

A proprietary **RAW** format file from a particular manufacturer may not be available in the future, making it difficult to use and exchange data between image editors. Is it worth storing your photos in a specific **RAW** format, and years later may be no longer supported by the manufacturer?

What's interesting about the **DNG** format is that, in addition to this proposal to maintain future compatibility, it is the encapsulation of various information about a photograph and, especially, its later editings. Thus, editing a photo in Lightroom or Camera RAW software and then exporting it in **DNG** means that all edits you make will be included along with the photo data itself, ie, its metadata, without the need for backing files. If a photo were initially edited in **JPEG** format, when it is saved in **DNG**, the new file would contain all edits made as well as their metadata. Each time you open this **DNG** file in Lightroom software, **Camera RAW**, or another image editor that supports this format, it will be in the same editings as when it was last exported. Better yet, you can change your edits again.

Observe in **figure 5.6**, located on the next page, a photograph in **DNG** format opened in the **Adobe Camera RAW** application. Note that in the panel on the right side of the window, highlighted in red, previously edited edits were automatically retrieved. That is, it is possible to encapsulate the edits made and the photo metadata in **DNG** files, which makes them very practical.

These features make the **DNG** format an exciting alternative to other formats, as it maintains future compatibility and allows more consistent file exchange. It is the most convenient way to archive your originals, as well as to store the photos themselves with their metadata.

This format brings together all edits made in a simple, easy-to-handle package that can be manipulated, used, and shared with compatible image editing softwares.

5.6 - DNG format image opened in Adobe Camera RAW application

Another exciting feature is that the format generates smaller files than **RAW**, about 80% of its original size. So converting your **RAW**-to-**DNG** photos right after **Importing** into the Lightroom software is a good idea as it saves computer memory space. However, like **RAW**, **DNG** files are still large files, unlike **JPEG** and other formats with data compression.

One thing to note is that, in principle, when converting to **DNG** format, the original **RAW** file data is lost. If you need to open the **RAW** file again in the original manufacturer application, this will no longer be possible.

To keep the original **RAW** file embedded in **DNG** during the photograph **Import** phase for future extraction, select the **Embed Original Raw File** checkbox on the **File Handling** tab of the Lightroom software **Preferences** window, which you can access through the menu. **Lightroom > Preferences...** or using the **Command + ,** shortcut key (**Ctrl + ,** in Windows). **Figure 5.7** presents the **Preferences** window with this option highlighted in red.

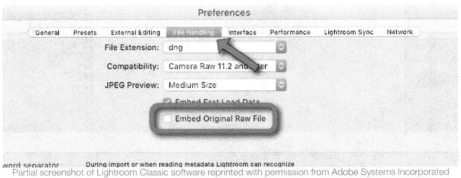

5.7 - Embed original raw file option from the Preferences window

Of course, this option will further increase the file size. Therefore, verify the real need to embed the **RAW** file in **DNG**. Also, remember that in the case of **JPEG** photos, converting them to **DNG** format should consume much more computer memory space.

5.1.4 - PSD Format

PSD is the format of files created by the Adobe Photoshop CC software, in which you can store all layers, masks, objects, vectors, and other components you build. Their extension is "**.psd**," and they are usually large files compared to other formats, especially when using many layers with various edits and sophisticated compositions.

The best way to open a file in **PSD** format is with the Adobe Photoshop CC software itself, thus maintaining full compatibility and feature availability. Given the popularity of this application, the format has good compatibility with other image editing programs, which are often able to import it with virtually all its features, although the results are not always the best in this case. The **PSD** accepts transparencies and is the ideal format for saving and editing jobs made in the Adobe Photoshop CC software, as it securely preserves all edits, layers, masks, etc.

You can import images in **PSD** format directly into the Lightroom software. Besides, a photo that already exists in your **Catalog** can be temporarily opened in the Adobe Photoshop CC software using the external editing feature, very conveniently due to the integration between the two programs. After advanced editing in the Adobe Photoshop CC software, you can easily return to the Lightroom software with built-in modifications.

The **PSD** format has no compression, thus maintaining the original quality of photos. It is particularly recommended for complex in-app layer edits where multiple photographs are creatively merged or when sophisticated adjustments to an image are required.

5.1.5 - TIFF Format

TIFF stands for *Tagged Image File Format*, being a very popular file format in image editing programs and scanners, as well as for image exchange between editors without loss of quality. Its file extension is "**.tiff**" or "**.tif**".

Because it has no compression, it generates large files that consume a lot of internal computer space, but favor the exchange of images between editors precisely because it does not degrade the original quality and has high portability.

It can store high definition colors if required using 32-bit color depth. Another essential feature is that it supports huge image files, up to 4 Gb, when most other formats, including the **PSD** from Adobe Photoshop CC software, only support up to 2 Gb.

Note:

*For files larger than 2 Gb, the Adobe Photoshop CC software lets you save your files in a specific format called "**Large Document Format**," whose extension is "**.psb**."*

Thus, it is a format that allows high compatibility, being recognized in practically all image editors and operating systems. It also supports transparencies and can store layers, which further facilitates file transfer between image editing programs, ensuring excellent portability.

5.1.6 - PNG Format

PNG stands for *Portable Network Graphics*. It is a format with compression but little quality loss and is widely used on the Internet. Its filename extension is ".**png**." Being a format that accepts up to 24-bits of color depth, it has excellent quality for photos, allowing smooth gradations of color and tones, with the possibility of using transparencies, which is not possible in **JPEG**.

By maintaining excellent quality in image files, it usually generates large files, which can be bypassed using the 8-bit color depth option. It produces smaller but lower quality files.

It is a format that has high compatibility with image editing programs, operating systems, and the Internet, which makes it suitable for excellent photo quality with the possibility of compression, but without limiting the absence of **JPEG** transparencies.

5.1.7 - GIF Format

GIF stands for *Graphics Interchange Format*, widely used on the Internet for displaying images with little solid colors and small animations, making it a very popular format on websites on this network. Its file extension is ".**gif**."

Because it is an 8-bit color depth format, it can only display up to 256 colors, making your files tiny and easy to upload over the Internet, hence its popularity, especially at the beginning of the World Wide Web. At that time, the slow transfer speeds of the file network did not allow the loading of heavy images in a reasonable time.

Another exciting feature of the format is that it can store several images in a single file, allowing you to create simple and easy to encapsulate and transmit animations, but without many features, such as the absence of audio, for example.

GIF supports transparencies and has high Internet compatibility and is suitable for images with large areas of solid color and few color variations as they are evident due to their limited number of colors. For the same reason, it is not suitable for photographic images due to the reduction in final quality.

Figure 5.8 shows the magnification of a portion of a cloud photograph in **GIF** format. Note that limiting the number of colors does not allow a smooth transition of image tones. Therefore, if you are going to use this format for photographs for some reason, which is not indicated, prefer low-color images and tonal gradations.

5.8 - Cloud Image in GIF Format

Probably due to these features, the Lightroom software does not support the **GIF** format, which focuses on photo editing. If you want to export a photo in this format, use the Adobe Photoshop CC software. With it, you can even determine the number of colors to be used in export, limited to 256 colors.

If you need to import a **GIF** format image into the Lightroom software, open it in another image editing application and export it in one of the supported formats. However, this new file will not make the quality of the photo better. And indeed, the editings in the Lightroom software will be very limited.

5.2 - When using RAW format on the camera

Cameras, especially professional and semi-professional ones, generally allow capturing images in **JPEG** and **RAW** formats, and more recently, **DNG**. Since **DNG** has virtually the same functionality as **RAW**, and is not yet directly available on most cameras, only **RAW** and **JPEG** will be covered in this topic.

The **RAW** format is better when maximum flexibility in image editing is desired, allowing for greater creativity and precise adjustments by the photographer. Because it is the format that stores the most information captured by the camera sensor, it also enables you to get the best photographic quality after editing.

Also, it is the format that allows you to retrieve the most information in the bright (overexposed) and dark (underexposed) areas of a photograph. It is not widely possible with such a **JPEG** format due to the discarding of information for file compression.

Another great advantage of the format is that the photographer can easily correct the **White Balance** in **Post-production**, as the file is not processed on camera, freeing it from further concern when capturing photographs. Even errors in the exposure are less worrying, given that the potential for future corrections to **RAW** files is much higher.

If you are shooting professionally, or if you are an amateur but want the best possible results, use the **RAW** format whenever possible, especially when high-end quality work and extensive creative possibilities are required. But be aware of the availability of memory card space and time constraints for exporting and sharing photos, as unlike **JPEG**, the **RAW** file needs to be processed to become a usable and shareable image.

The **RAW** file format is, therefore, best suited for photo editing in the Lightroom software. Whenever possible, make your photographs using this format. The **DNG** format is also a great alternative to **RAW** in cameras where it is available.

5.3 - When using JPEG format on the camera

Despite compression losses, the **JPEG** format is widely used because it is practical, very small compared to **RAW** or **DNG**, and highly compatible with all image editing programs, computer operating systems and mobile devices, and also with the Internet.

Despite compression, it maintains good quality in photographic images when kept at low compressions, which still considerably reduces file size. The practicality is due to the previous camera's "development" itself that, depending on the purpose, may even dispense with further editing. The file is ready to be printed or shared if you do not have many image quality requirements.

The vast majority of cameras and even the latest smartphones have simple **Post-production** features built-in, though very limited compared to Adobe Photoshop CC or Lightroom software. It is especially relevant when it is necessary to quickly forward images over the Internet such as journalists, or in everyday situations. For example, when you want to share the best photos of your unforgettable birthday party quickly.

Nowadays, due to the popularization of social networks, there seems to be a need for almost immediate sharing of photographs of social events, prioritizing the speed of posting rather than the quality of images. In these cases, **JPEG** fits perfectly as the best option. Importantly, the Lightroom and Adobe Photoshop CC software have mobile versions allowing, with some limitations concerning their desktop versions, the editing of photos on the device itself and where they were captured. Browse your smartphone or tablet operating system online store to download the mobile versions of these applications and others available from Adobe. The results of these edits are very good and can provide superior quality to your shared images directly from mobile devices.

The file size is one more reason to choose **JPEG**. If there are too many photos to capture and too little memory card space, it is good to stay away from **RAW** as the work may be incomplete.

Another advantage of **JPEG** is that, in the case of fast-sequence shooting, the camera will usually be available for the next click faster when shooting in **JPEG** than in **RAW**, given the file size. In the latter format, the time taken to write data to the memory card is longer. It is particularly relevant in action photography, such as sporting events or bird flights, where a quick sequence of photographs is required to select the best one later. Birds in flight and athletes in action do not stop in front of the camera and pose while being photographed. Professional cameras usually record faster, but even so, the file format can limit the capture speed in high-speed sequences.

Thus, sometimes speed is better than quality, avoiding losing that extraordinary photograph by waiting for the camera to be ready for the next photo, or a delay in sharing due to the need to "develop" a **RAW** file. Instead, use **JPEG** when practicality, lower memory consumption, and speed are more relevant factors than photo quality and **Post-production** flexibility.

Importantly, despite the maximum quality and flexibility of images taken with **RAW** files, currently, **JPEG** photos are also very good quality, depending on the characteristics of your camera and its correct setting at the time of the shooting. The choice of format will depend on the photographer's goal.

5.4 - When to use other formats

RAW and **JPEG** are the formats commonly used by cameras for recording images captured by the sensor. However, the Lightroom software and other editing applications support different formats, either at **Import** or after editing is complete, when photos are finally exported or shared.

The choice of the final format of a photograph will depend on the purpose of your work. To print, view on your computer, share on the Internet, create compositions, and other purposes, you should choose the most appropriate format. It is, therefore, essential to know the main formats and their characteristics, as well as to be able to compare them to choose the best option. You should try to avoid using a single format because it may have limitations, depending on your purpose.

5.5 - Comparative table of image formats

To facilitate the choice of the best image file format according to the intended final result, the worksheet of **figure 5.9**, which presents a comparative table of the main formats discussed above and their main characteristics, was prepared as a reference suggestion.

	JPEG	RAW	DNG	PSD	TIFF	PNG	GIF
Use in photography	Yes	Yes	Yes	Yes	Yes	Yes	No
Compatibility with other software	High	Low	Low	Medium	High	High	High
File size	Medium	Large	Large	Large	Large	Medium	Small
Data compression	Yes	No	No	No	No	Yes	No
Loss of photographic quality	Yes	No	No	No	No	Yes	Yes
Transparency compatible	No	No	No	Yes	Yes	Yes	Yes
Compositions with layers	No	No	No	Yes	Yes	No	No
Images with many tones	Good	Excellent	Excellent	Excellent	Excellent	Good	Bad
Images with many solid colors	Good	Good	Good	Good	Good	Good	Excellent
Printings with many tones	Good	-	-	Excellent	Excellent	Good	Bad
Sharing on the Internet	Excellent	-	-	-	Bad	Excellent	Excellent
Sharing among editors	Excellent	Bad	Good	Excellent	Excellent	Excellent	Good

5.9 - Comparison chart between image formats

Smart Tips!

Tip #10 - Importing in DNG Format

If you want to convert all **RAW** files to **DNG**, please be aware that you can do this during the **Import** photographs process into the Lightroom software. Just select **Copy as DNG** from the available options (**figure 5.10**). This subject will be covered in more detail in **Chapter 7 - Importing and Organizing of Photographs**, located in **Volume #2** of the **Editing and Management of Photographs** series.

Partial screenshot of Lightroom Classic software reprinted with permission from Adobe Systems Incorporated

5.10 - Copy as DNG command while importing images

Tip #11 - Embed the RAW File in DNG

You can embed the **RAW** file in **DNG** by exporting it in the Lightroom software. This way, the **RAW** file will not be discarded. It can be extracted from the **DNG** in the future if you wish to reopen it in the original **RAW** format reader application provided by the camera manufacturer. This subject will be covered in more detail in **Chapter 19 - Exporting and Sharing Photographs**, located in **Volume #10** of the **Editing and Management of Photographs** series.

Tip #12 - Shoot in Two Formats Simultaneously

Some cameras, usually semi-professional and professional cameras, allow you to capture **RAW** and **JPEG** photographs simultaneously, generating two files for each photo. For fast-forwarding or sharing, you can use **JPEG** images immediately, and those that can be processed with more time and detail can be edited from the **RAW** file. Keep in mind the increased recording time of files in the camera, and you will need a memory card with good capacity depending on the number of photos to create two files for each one.

Tip #13 - Shoot in Two Formats Simultaneously #2

Another advantage of simultaneously shooting in two formats is the time that can be reduced in editing if there are many images to be processed. **JPEG** photos that have been well treated by the camera may not need editing, making the process quicker. Those whose **JPEG** results were not to their liking may be edited in **RAW** format, allowing for greater possibilities for correction. The same is true for artistic creations with the image, as **RAW** will allow more flexibility. Check your camera's manual to see if it has **RAW** and **JPEG** simultaneous recording capability, and how to turn it on.

Tip #14 - DNG Converter

Adobe provides a **DNG** file converter software called Adobe® DNG Converter (**figure 5.11**, located on the next page). With it, you can convert **RAW** files to **DNG**, including embedding it in **DNG** if desired. Conversely, you can also extract **RAW** files from embedded **DNG**.

5.11 - Adobe DNG Converter software

Tip #15 - Enhancing Camera Development

To make the **RAW-JPEG** format camera "develop" as close as possible to the desired result, use the camera's available setup features. In the case of the Nikon D7100, for example, the function is called **Picture Control**, which allows for various development settings such as **SD Standard, Neutral NL, Vivid VI, MC Monochrome, PT Portrait**, and **LS Landscape**. If you are photographing a children's party, a good option may be **VI Vivid**, to highlight the many intense colors present in this type of event. If it's a landscape, try **LS Landscape** mode, and if you shoot a face, try **PT Portrait** to soften skin tones and reduce the depth of field. Check your camera's manual for the availability of this feature or similar feature and how to set it up. On some more advanced cameras, you can even set up custom **Picture Controls** and save them for later use. The feature is handy and will allow you to get much more accurate "development" of **JPEG** photos as expected by the photographer.

Note:

*Do not confuse the **Picture Control feature** in **Tip #15** with the **Scene Modes** of the camera, whose names are similar. These modes, which exist on most cameras, including compact cameras and even smartphones, allow automatic settings for a particular type of scene to be photographed, such as **Portraits**, **Landscapes**, **Sports**, **Macro**, etc. These **Scene Modes** enable you to automatically adjust aperture, speed, ISO, etc., depending on the subject you want to shoot and the ambient lighting conditions obtained by the camera's photometer. Therefore, these **Scene Modes** will influence the image data captured by the camera sensor, whatever mode is chosen. **Picture Control**, in turn, will only work on "developing" the picture, ie, the final processing by the camera to make it **JPEG**.*

Tip #16 - JPEG on Camera Viewfinder

When shooting with the **RAW** format, the camera will make a "development" in **JPEG** so that it can be shown on its small **LCD** screen and allows for a preview of the photograph. If you select a **Picture Control** on the camera, the **JPEG** preview image will display the result with this setting on the **LCD**. But do not rely too much on this image, because the influence of ambient light can lead the photographer to misinterpret photography, whether in **White Balance**, exposure, or even color saturation. Previewing photography is a handy feature and a radical change from the old analog process of film photography when the result could only be verified after paper development. Thus, once again, the RAW format will be of great help in these cases as further adjustments can be made much more flexibly in **Post-production**.

Note:

*If the camera does not have **Picture Control**, when sensor data is "developed" to **JPEG**, it will make a default development based on the captured image data. If you capture the picture in **RAW** format only, **Picture Control** will not influence these files as **RAW** preserves the original data obtained by the camera sensor without any processing. Only the **JPEG** image displayed as a preview of the photograph on the camera's LCD screen or computer file manager (image thumbnail) will have been processed. However, this processing will not be saved if the camera has been configured to record photographs in **RAW** only.*

Review

Answer the questions below to consolidate the knowledge gained. The answers are in the **Appendix - Exercise Answers**.

1) What is the image file format most often found in digital still cameras?

a) GIF
b) RAW
c) PSD
d) JPEG
e) DOCX

2) What is the image file format that stores all data obtained by the sensor of a digital still camera?

a) XLS
b) RAW
c) PNG
d) TIFF
e) PSB

3) What is the negative consequence of using compression in image file formats that provide this option?

a) Reduction of the image file name
b) Increased file size
c) Reduced image exchange compatibility
d) File extension change and consequent transmission difficulty
e) Loss of image data and consequent quality reduction

4) Why are successive editing and saving of JPEG images not recommended?

a) Change the original file name definitively
b) Reduce their compatibility in case of successive rescues
c) Cause progressive loss of quality with each file save
d) Initial changes are always lost
e) No successive editing in JPEG files possible

5) What is the name of the application launched automatically by the Adobe Photoshop CC software when opening a RAW format file?

a) Adobe DNG converter
b) RAW converter
c) Adobe Lightroom Classic
d) Adobe Camera RAW
e) Open RAW

6) What is data file format considered the digital equivalent of the old film negative, usually found in semi-professional and professional cameras?

a) GIF
b) XML

c) RAW
d) TIF
e) PSD

7) What is the file format that was created to maintain the future compatibility of images captured in the RAW format?

a) DNG
b) GIF
c) JPEG
d) NEF
e) CR2

8) Regarding the PSD file format, tick the INCORRECT alternative:

a) Has medium compatibility with other image editing programs
b) Stores the created layers
c) Generates large files due to the complexity of the compositions
d) Accepts transparencies and PNG export
e) Can edit files larger than 3 Gb in size

9) What is the name of the image file format that is very popular in scanner-type equipment, which allows the exchange of images between editors without degrading the quality of the original?

a) DNG
b) PSD
c) TIFF
d) GIF
e) TXT

10) Which image file format has good color depth, with the possibility of using transparencies,

and is very popular on the Internet for photo sharing?

a) GIF
b) PNG
c) JPEG
d) EXE
e) TIFF

11) What is the name of the file format that is very popular on the Internet, especially at the beginning of the World Wide Web (www), due to the low transfer rates of the network at the time, and which is suitable for images with many solid colors and few tone graduations?

a) GIF
b) PNG
c) DNG
d) TIFF
e) RAW

12) What file format should be used with the camera if you want great flexibility in retrieving photo information, especially in bright and dark areas?

a) JPEG
b) GIF
c) TIFF
d) RAW
e) PNG

13) What is the file format to use for cameras when you want to share a photo quickly?

a) DNG
b) TIFF

c) GIF
d) LOP
e) JPEG

14) **Which file format should be avoided for photographs due to their low color availability?**

a) RAW
b) PSD
c) TIF
d) JPEG
e) GIF

15) **Which of the following allows you to import a RAW photo file into the Lightroom application, automatically converting it to DNG?**

a) Add DNG
b) Move
c) Convert to DNG
d) Copy as DNG
e) Import DNG

16) **Which file format allows you to embed a RAW file, allowing it to be extracted in the future?**

a) DNG
b) GIF
c) FOT
d) JPEG
e) TIF

Important Notes:

Chapter 6

Lightroom Software Workflow

The beginning, middle, and end of a process

Chapter 4 - Photography Workflow presented a generic process suggestion for a photographic activity, from the **Planning** phase to the end of the process, in the **Archiving** phase.

This chapter will present a **Workflow** using the Lightroom software in the **Post-production** and the **Export and Sharing** phases in **Photography Workflow**. These are the phases most directly related to using the software. It is important to emphasize that it can also be used as a backup tool in the **Production** phase, through the **Tethered Capture** tool (see **Smart Tip #17**), and in the **Archiving** phase using the photo catalog management and configuration features.

As presented in the **Photography Workflow**, the flow proposed in this chapter for the Lightroom software is just a suggestion based on the author's experience using the app. Each photographer develops their workflow, according to their specific needs and personal way of working. This chapter's purpose is to present a starting point for beginners and possibilities for improvement for those already experienced in the subject.

Objectives of the chapter:

- ‣ emphasize the importance of backups;
- ‣ submit a **Workflow** proposal in the Lightroom software; and
- ‣ show an overview of the process.

6.1 - Importance of Workflow in Lightroom Application

In any human activity, it is possible to accomplish a particular task in countless ways, achieving the same results. What sets them apart is the path found, which can be simpler or more complex, more economical, or more expensive, faster, or longer. This path is the process to follow.

One should always strive to perfect a **Process** in the light of experiences gained from the permanent goal of doing better with less time and resources. In photography, it is no different, especially in the so-called **Post-production** phase, where the use of an editing program can be more or less productive depending on the process the user adopts about its use.

The Lightroom software has its focus on productivity. And that is one of its greatest virtues. If used together with a consistent process, it is possible to produce excellent results quickly, which would be difficult without their use. So before we start using the Lightroom software itself, it's essential to review a **Workflow** for your job, making the most of its capabilities.

6.2 - Backup of photographic archives

As noted in the **Post-production** phase in **Chapter 4 - Photography Workflow,** it is crucial to back up before starting any work in the Lightroom software. It is not difficult to lose all jobs by carelessness. The app itself has the capabilities to back-up during photo **Import**, a topic to be covered in detail in **Chapter 7 - Importing and Organizing of Photographs,** located in **Volume #2** of the **Editing and Management of Photographs** series.

Just start your **Workflow** in the Lightroom software with **Backups** ready, before moving on to the next steps. To do this, read the backup suggestions in **Chapter 4 - Photography Workflow** as needed until you get used to this process. This way, the chances of losing all your work are significantly reduced so that you can proceed with peace of mind.

6.3 - Lightroom Workflow Steps

The steps listed below are a good starting point for using the Lightroom software productively. You should always strive to refine the **Process** to meet your specific needs and personal way of working as you get used to the application.

If you are a novice user, I suggest that you print the **Workflow Overview** flowchart page at the end of this chapter for easy reference while using the application.

The **Lightroom Software Workflow** proposed in this book has six phases:

- ▸ Cataloging;
- ▸ Importing;
- ▸ Selecting and Rating;
- ▸ Editing;
- ▸ Exporting and Sharing; and
- ▸ Archiving.

The following stages of this process will be presented below.

6.3.1 - Cataloging

After backing up, the first step in the **Process** concerns is cataloging. A **Catalog** is a database created by the Lightroom software to store photographs, their data, and their edits, all transparently and practically for the user, who rarely has to worry about locating files while using the program. And even if you try, it will be difficult because the traditional **Open**, **Save**, and **Save As** commands, for example, don't exist in the Lightroom software.

Only at the end of the process will you need to set a location for **Exporting** photos if you want to generate new image files on your hard drive, but even then, depending on the desired output, this may not be necessary. It is the case for e-mail and social sharing, for example, in which edited photos will be published directly, without having to export the edited file to the computer hard drive or other storage media.

There are different ways to handle the **Catalog** in the Lightroom software. You can manage all photos in the same **Catalog**, or you can create new catalogs if you feel it is convenient. The first time you run the program on your computer, it creates a default **Catalog** itself that you can continue to use. Alternatively, you can also define a new one according to your specific needs, which is recommended.

Chapter 7 - Importing and Organizing of Photographs, located in **Volume #2** of the **Editing and Management of Photographs** series, will cover all of these possibilities in detail. For now, the critical thing to keep in mind is that after backing up, choosing the **Catalog** and its settings is the starting point for a good Lightroom software **Workflow**.

6.3.2 - Importing

Created the database that will manage your work, called **Catalog**, it is necessary to bring into it the photographs to be stored and edited, an essential task of the **Importing** phase. If you prefer, and depending on the situation, you can bring the images into the Lightroom software without actually copying them, creating only links between the **Catalog** and the location of the files on your computer.

Importing enables numerous configurations. It is a significant step in the future management of photographs, as well as the consistency of their storage, going far beyond merely bringing the images into the **Catalog**.

Chapter 7 - Importing and Organizing of Photographs, located in **Volume #2** of the **Editing and Management of Photographs** series, will cover this subject in more detail. For now, it is essential to understand that **Cataloging** and **Importing** will be the phases responsible for the storage structure of photographs that will support the next steps.

6.3.3 - Selecting and Rating

Every photographer knows that after the **Production** phase, countless photos will be available, but not all will be used. Some will be rejected, either because they have uncorrectable problems, such as an entirely blurred image, or even because only a few photographs are required, which will be selected from the available ones. Also, it is important to classify the pictures according to some of the parameters available in the software.

The Lightroom software has a true arsenal of tools available for selecting and marking photos in catalogs, making this step very productive for the facilities offered to the user.

Only after **Selecting** should you proceed to the next step, when only the selected or sorted photos will be edited, without deleting the others from the hard drive. As already mentioned, you will rarely have to worry about directories and files when working with the Lightroom software. Further details on **Selecting** and **Marking** of photographs will be covered in **Chapter 9 - Marking and Selecting of Photographs**, located in **Volume #3** of the **Editing and Management of Photographs** series.

6.3.4 - Editing

After cataloging, importing, selecting, and classifying the photographs, we can then edit them to "correct their imperfections" or create artistic modifications.

Note:

> The expression "correct their imperfections" should be understood as the corrections to be eventually made to the photograph to bring it closer to the image captured by the photographer's eyes at the moment of capture, with minimal loss of information in the picture. We seek to correct technical aspects such as **White Balance**, **Exposure**, **Contrast**, etc. However, this is a subjective matter as these corrections are never identical when performed by different people. Also, the photographer's intent often may require a seemingly "imperfect" photo, depending on his or her purpose. A photograph with a poorly lit person against a bright background, for example, can be viewed as an exposure problem or, if the photographer intended, as an artistic image of a silhouette against a well-lit background. Another classic example is a slightly yellowish indicating a tropical and warm location, in which case the **White Balance** "correction" could impoverish the result in relation to the photographer's objective.

At this stage, much of the work will be done in the software, using its various panels and features that can retrieve unattractive photographs, and modify them to obtain the most varied results.

Beginning with **Chapter 11 - Basic Photographs Editing**, located in **Volume #4** of the **Editing and Management of Photographs** series, several chapters will introduce you to the features and tools of the Lightroom software for handling photo editing, which is usually the most complex and time-consuming part of the process.

6.3.5 - Exporting and Sharing

After finishing the editing of the photographs, it is time to get the final product of all the work done. For this, new photos can be generated in various formats for saving to the hard disk, or share them directly on social networks, by email or with the other options available in the program.

One of the significant advantages of Lightroom software in the productivity issue appears in this phase, because it is possible to **Export** and **Share** all the edited photos in batch, without the need of commands like **Save** and its consequent opening of configuration windows. Select the desired format type and output settings. So, the application will take the necessary actions for all selected photographs. And most importantly, it happens in the background. That is, you do not have to wait for the application to finish the exporting or sharing task, as you can keep working while they happen in the background at the same time.

You can even perform more than one **Exporting** or **Sharing** task simultaneously. You can, for example, export your photos at 300 dpi for future printing and at the same time, share the same images on social networks before you complete the previous job.

And while all this happens, you can continue to use the software without any problems, as ongoing tasks will continue to be done in the background. It is a good example of how Lightroom software is very productive when compared to other image editing programs. These aspects will be covered in more depth in **Chapter 19 - Exporting and Sharing of Photographs**, located in **Volume #10** of the **Editing and Management of Photographs** series.

6.3.6 - Archiving

An important step in the **Lightroom Workflow** is the final archiving of the work done. As we will see in the next volumes of the **Editing and Management of Photographs** series, it is not always necessary to have all photos forever in the same **Catalog** on your computer hard drive. For professional photographers, **Archiving** is even more critical because of the future possibility of new uses for old client archives or the photographer himself. Likewise, amateur photographers will eventually be able to create sets of photographs that will not be immediately usable, so **Archiving** is required to preserve their image bank.

It's important to mention that the Lightroom software is designed to manage large photo catalogs. Nothing prevents you from continuing to use all of your photos in one **Catalog**, but depending on their purpose, it may be interesting to store them elsewhere. Especially for professional photographers who need to keep large quantities of customer photos in high resolution, it may be that in addition to having a huge **Catalog**, the hard disk space of the computer starts to be a problem.

Archiving is a task that can be accomplished in many different ways, depending on the specific needs of each user. The **Cataloging** and **Importing** phases are directly related to the **Archiving** step since they will be the ones that will previously define the location of the **Catalog** files and the structure of files and folders in which the original photographs will be stored in the computer.

Because of this, **Archiving** should be considered early in the **Process**, although it is effectively done as the last step of the workflow, as we will see in future chapters. Archiving will be covered in more detail in **Chapter 20 - Archiving**, located in **Volume #11** of the **Editing and Management of Photographs** series.

6.4 - Lightroom Application Workflow Overview

The flowchart in **figure 6.1** presents the **Lightroom Software Workflow** proposed by the author. It is suggested to print this page until the **Process** is well consolidated by use.

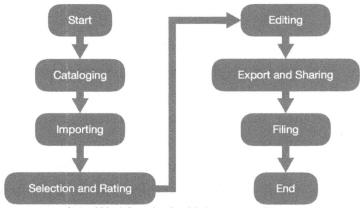

6.1 - Workflow in the Lightroom software

Note that the **Post-production** phase in **Photography Workflow**, as well as **Exporting** and **Sharing** phases, can be entirely achieved in the Lightroom software itself. Other steps, such as **Production** and **Archiving**, also have tasks that can be performed with the support of tools included in the program, such as **Tethered Capture** in the **Production** phase, and **Exporting** and **Catalog Backup** in the **Archiving** phase.

Smart Tips!

Tip #17 - Tethered Capture

Tethered Capture allows the photographer to capture photos directly from the camera to the computer using the Lightroom software, which is especially useful for studio work. The program allows this type of capture in the **Production** phase by transferring the photos directly to your **Catalog** or a specific folder on your computer hard drive. It is possible through a floating window with commands that allow the camera to be triggered remotely. Note in **figure 6.2** that the camera connected in this example is a Nikon D7100 (left side of the window), and the floating window displays some camera settings in, such as **Speed, Aperture, ISO** number, and **White Balance**. To shoot, click the large round button located on the right side of the floating window. Access this feature from the **File menu > Tethered Capture > Start Tethered Capture...**

Partial screenshot of Lightroom Classic app reprinted with permission from Adobe Systems Incorporated

6.2 - Tethered Capture floating window

Tip #18 - Camera Pre-Selection

During the **Production** phase, there may be situations where the photographer has a reasonable amount of time available waiting for the moment to re-capture photographs. It may be, for example, that you are waiting for the best sunset time to photograph or, at a social event, are just waiting for speeches to produce more photos. In this waiting time, it is interesting to review the photos in the camera and already delete those that are useless. This way, you can save memory card space and time in the **Post-production** phase. But be careful and only do so if you really have time to do the task calmly and with concentration so that you do not unduly delete photographs. Cameras usually ask for confirmation, but once the command is executed, the image is permanently deleted from the card.

Review

Answer the questions below to consolidate the knowledge gained. The answers are in the **Appendix - Exercise Answers**.

1) Which steps of Photography Workflow are most directly related to using the Lightroom software?

a) Planning / Archiving
b) Production / Exporting
c) Post-production / Distribution and Sharing
d) Selecting / Importing
e) Post-production / Exporting and Sharing

2) The Lightroom software can be used in the Photography Workflow Production phase using which tool?

a) Linked Capture
b) Background Analyzer
c) Splitting and Mirroring Tool
d) Mode selector
e) Layer Analyzer

3) What is the user advisable to do before starting any new work on the Lightroom software?

a) Save your files in the program
b) Backing up your original photographs
c) Set up the Adobe Photoshop CC software
d) Select the best photos
e) Create a new Catalog

4) What is the Lightroom software database called where photographs, metadata, and edits are stored?

a) Workspace
b) Paste
c) Library
d) Collection
e) Catalog

5) At which phase of the Lightroom Software Workflow is most of the work done, such as White Balance and Exposure correction?

a) Export
b) Planning
c) Editing
d) Cleaning the lens
e) Cataloging

6) In the Lightroom Workflow, which phases are most related to the Archiving phase, due to the physical location of the Catalog files and the original photographs?

a) Exporting and Editing
b) Cataloging and Importing
c) Editing and Importing
d) Sharing and Selecting
e) Cataloging and Editing

Important Notes:

Volume #2 of Editing and Management of Photograph Series

We have reached the end of the first volume of the **Editing and Management of Photographs** series. In **Volume #2 - Importing and Organizing of Photographs,** you'll learn all the steps and settings you need to efficiently and securely import and organize your photos in the Lightroom software. These steps are the first steps to a consistent application workflow.

All volumes in the series feature full text on the subject matter in the title of each book and numerous screenshots of the Lightroom software to enable you to learn even without your computer. Besides, answer-fixing exercises, shortcuts lists, and smart tips are available throughout the work. See you there in **Volume #2**! It is coming soon!

Volume #2 - Importing and Organizing of Photographs

The **Volume #2 - Importing and Organizing of Photographs** has one chapter:

- ▸ Chapter 7 - Importing and Organizing of Photographs;
- ▸ Smart Tips!
- ▸ Shortcuts;
- ▸ Review Exercises; and
- ▸ Appendix - Exercise Answers.

Appendix - Exercise Answers

Volume #1 - Basic Concepts and Workspace

Chapter	Question															
	1	2	3	4	5	6	7	8	9	10	11	12	13	14	15	16
1	D	B	A	E	C	B	D	D	C	C	-	-	-	-	-	-
2	C	E	A	-	-	-	-	-	-	-	-	-	-	-	-	-
3	B	E	A	B	E	D	C	E	C	A	B	C	A	-	-	-
4	D	B	E	B	E	B	A	C	A	C	A	D	B	-	-	-
5	D	B	E	C	D	C	A	E	C	B	A	D	E	E	D	A
6	E	A	B	E	C	B	-	-	-	-	-	-	-	-	-	-

About the author

J. Armando Fernandes is Brazilian and for many years, has been practicing photography and filming as hobbies have taken seriously in his spare time. He currently works as a Photographer and Image Editor, using the Adobe Photoshop Lightroom Classic and Adobe Photoshop CC software. Besides, he has courses in Digital Photography and Graphic Design at SENAC. Most recently, he also writes books and publishes his photographs in online image banks.

www.ingramcontent.com/pod-product-compliance
Lightning Source LLC
Chambersburg PA
CBHW071132050326
40690CB00008B/1439